To Marg—,

Stories from the Front Lines

The Battle Against Abortion

We will end abortion!

JUDY MADSEN JOHNSON

Matthew 25:40

ISBN: 1495213137
ISBN-13: 978-1495213137

Published by EA Books, Inc.
www.eabooksonline.com

ENDORSEMENTS

"God bless Judy Madsen Johnson for writing *"Stories from the Front Lines."* In this book Judy highlights the effort of those dedicated to protecting the most valuable resource in our society–the unborn. Everyone who cares about the sanctity of life should read this compelling volume."

Dr. Robert Jeffress, Senior Pastor, First Baptist Church, Dallas TX

"To vanquish a great injustice, it takes a variety of diligent, deeply convicted, sometimes controversial people to expose and confront the evil. Judy Madsen Johnson has given historians a gift, that will also prod readers– especially Christians–to discover ways to confront modern-day evils like abortion."

Wendy Wright, Vice President for Government Communications and Relations, C-FAM, New York NY

"Abortion is the greatest atrocity, the most horrific evil this country has ever seen. Thank God for those who have the courage to speak up for those who cannot speak for themselves. As a stalwart of the Pro-Life Movement, Judy Madsen Johnson has done us all a great service by compiling the most comprehensive and diverse collection of articles currently available by men and women committed to uphold the value of every precious God-given life. These articles will not only inform and enlighten, but also inspire you to take action: to pray, to speak, and to show others there is a better way."

Rev. Frank Cavalli, Senior Pastor, St. Paul's Presbyterian Church, Orlando FL

"Judy Madsen Johnson has been a tireless voice for the pre-born. I had the privilege of representing her before the United States Supreme Court in the case of Madsen v. Women's Health Center, an abortion clinic which ceased operations years ago. It is impossible to comprehend the widespread destruction caused by abortion. It brutally kills innocent children, hurts women, perverts motherhood and fatherhood, and spreads its tentacles of pain throughout our society. We cannot remain silent in the midst of this tragic holocaust. Each of us will be held accountable for our actions or inactions in the face of this horrible genocide. One person can make a difference. The Church must rise up in this generation and we must return to a culture of life. *Stories from the Front Lines* is a must read."

Mathew D. Staver, Founder and Chairman, Liberty Counsel, VA, FL, DC

In Memory of Carole Griffin, 1938 – 2012

Election cycles come and go, but no matter who occupied their seat in Florida State Government, Carole Griffin knew them, and they knew her. Well liked and respected by both parties, everyone knew where she stood. She called governors by their first name.

Carole was a true champion for the unborn and she had the political expertise to see a task through. Many who went into "battle" with Carole were taught how to lobby and stay on point during press conferences. Her professional bearing and style kept her ready at a moment's notice.

Carole was a champion of freedom for Christian principles. Her tireless determination helped defeat ERA. She worked on behalf of the Home School bill, but her most pressing priority was protecting the unborn babies. She gave leadership to Right to Life and Eagle Forum. She broadcast her own radio show. There was no better source for news than Carole.

The passing of Carole is a loss for many privileged to have worked beside her. The things she cared for and was passionate about represented core Christian and American values. She left a void. We miss her.

In Memory of Nellie Gray, 1924 – 2012

Excerpts from *Washington Times*, August 20, 2012 editorial by Rep. Christopher H. Smith, NJ.

"At Nellie's first March for Life on Jan. 22, 1974, I, along with thousands of others, gathered in the nation's capital believing that the innate cruelty of *Roe v. Wade* would be rejected by compassionate Americans, including politicians. The great March for Life, hatched in her living room, went on to become the nation's largest annual pro-life gathering.

She never wavered from this goal, calling upon 'all grass-roots pro-lifers and government officials to unite because any abortion is untenable.' "

Nellie's life was characterized by service to her country. She served as a corporal in the Women's Army Corps in World War II and earned an undergraduate business degree, a master's degree in economics, and a law degree. She worked as a civil servant in the Departments of State and Labor for 28 years. She retired from the federal government early so that she could help lead the effort to restore legal protections to the preborn.

No matter whom she addressed—young marchers in the crowd or presidents of the United States—Nellie's message was clear, unambiguous, empathetic, and proudly pro-life.

In Memory of over Fifty-Six Million Missing Babies

The nine-week-old pre-born baby on the cover seemed to be pondering a future with a mommy and a daddy. He sucked his thumb. He could hear voices, music, and feel vibrations. In this moment he was safe, secure, comfortable in the most sacred place designed for a developing baby, his mother's womb.

And then came horrific, inescapable, death.

DEDICATION

Pat Harmon, Godmother to the Pre-born Babies

Pat Harmon is representative of other humble, selfless warriors of many years, standing against the killing of God's innocent ones. She and they shy from attention.

Shouts from passing cars, "Get a job," or "Don't you have anything better to do?" are probably heard outside every abortion clinic in America. No one has heard it more than Pat Harmon. The remark closest to hitting the mark is, "Haven't you got a life?" Yes, Pat has a life, and it's a day-after-day pursuit in her own way of saving a baby's life.

Excerpted here, Christopher Murphy's article on the editorial page of the *Orlando Sentinel*, October 25, 2011 described Pat best: "My destination required me to make a right on Virginia Drive where I saw, sitting on a small portable stool outside the EPOC Clinic, one older woman. She was holding flyers meant to discourage women from paying the clinic staff to kill their unborn daughters and sons.

The woman who has sat outside that clinic for years enjoys no police protection and no media attention. The woman is quiet, she is committed, and she likely will be out there as long as she's alive and mobile. Alone, unassuming, that woman has more guts and character than every occupier of every Wall Street on the planet. More important, a boy whose mother might have killed him will be laughing with joy as he drives in a run and arrives safe at first base in his Little League game."

A few years ago, Pat planned to attend the luncheon being held to benefit Pro-Life Action Ministries following her shift on the sidewalk. This ministry which furnishes pro-life materials, training, and volunteers to staff the sidewalks, was going to honor Pat publicly. However, Pat's partner had to leave due to a family member being hospitalized. Pat never budged from her post. Her seat at the luncheon table remained empty.

When we look for heroes to emulate, don't forget the example of one woman who lives life simply, devotedly, for the unborn babies. Her name is Pat Harmon.

ACKNOWLEDGEMENTS

Thank you to my Triune God who gave me this vision toward that wonderful day when every child, in the womb and outside the womb, will be safe, loved, and welcomed.

Thank you to those who have given permission for their chapters to be included in this collection. Their methods of pro-life activism often differ as they follow God's leading to exercise their unique and varied gifts. He sees the outcome. As their editor and fellow believer for the *sanctity of life*, I count it an extreme privilege to present their inspiring stories. This collection is by no means complete. There are many others who deserve recognition for their service for life. I exhort them to continue the written history of this great campaign until abortion has been abolished.

Thank you to EABooks whose President and Founder Cheri Cowell was editor of my first book, *Joy Cometh in the Morning, the Joy Postle Blackstone Story*. Her enthusiasm and expertise has convinced me to keep launching out.

A big thank-you also to my neighbor and proofreader, Linda Vail, who has been always available for my writing projects, offering helpful suggestions and my Word Weavers' Orlando Critique Group coaching and encouraging me; and my husband Mitch allowing me to take large chunks of time to produce this final manuscript.

CONTENTS

FOREWORD

When the telephone rang in my office that Friday afternoon in 2000, I had no idea how radically my life was about to change. The caller identified herself as Judy Madsen Johnson. Judy shared that she was contacting pastors in the area to see who would be interested in joining a pro-life prayer support group the next Saturday in front of an abortion clinic in Orlando. I accepted the invitation and for the next seven years I learned from Judy Johnson what being pro-life really means.

Many pastors today have a sermon or two they modify each year on Sanctity of Human Life Sunday to keep the pro-lifers in their congregations happy and fulfill their pro-life duty. I must admit that prior to Judy's phone call, I was one of them. But being able to live a pro-life adventure has meant more to me than one can imagine. I credit Judy Johnson as the primary instrument God the Holy Spirit has used in the formation of my convictions and leading me into this very worthy cause.

Judy taught me how to stand on a sidewalk in front of an abortion clinic in searing ninety-degree central Florida heat and cry out to those intent on aborting their pre-born children. She taught me:

- To stand fast in the face of threats and ridicule from those the prince of darkness places at the abortion clinic entrances to discourage us.
- The differences between simply having a pro-life preference and having a passion to save the pre-born from the ravages of abortion.
- That being pro-life involves more than just holding a sign, handing out literature, protesting, preaching a sermon, or picketing.
- Being pro-life goes to the center—the very DNA of one's character. Pro-life isn't just something we do, but a way of living, being, and influencing others as we honor and uphold the dignity and image of our God in the process.
- Being pro-life is not only rescuing the perishing but sharing God's love and His eternal hope with those about to make the gravest mistake of their lives.

Because of Judy's life and selfless devotion, I've witnessed how effectively and powerfully the Holy Spirit will speak through a person who is committed to following God's prompting in saving babies regardless of the cost. Judy's pro-life influence has resulted in countless decisions for life by young expectant mothers and continues even today in her roles as a writer and speaker, as she compassionately and articulately appeals to their God-given sense of motherhood.

Throughout those years, I also witnessed Judy's bold challenges to young men who nonchalantly meandered into the killing centers behind the young mothers—as if their duties were completed by bringing them to a doctor who could *fix* their problem. Judy's challenges to those young men still echo in my memory: *"Anyone can be a father, but a real man is a dad,"* Judy would say. Her words often stopped them in their tracks. No, they did not always come to the sidewalk and talk with us. But sometimes they did, and on occasion, they even re-entered the killing centers. They attempted to convince the expectant mothers to reconsider and hopefully, choose life for their child. Some left the killing centers with girlfriend or wife in hand, resolute in choosing life for their baby.

Judy's compassion for the unborn extended to those who worked in the clinics. She realized those employed in such a place undergo a dehumanizing process. Once, as I stood beside Judy on the sidewalk in front of a killing center, she spoke to an abortion worker arriving for the day. Leaving her car, the worker made her way toward the entrance of the clinic. As she had done so many times before, Judy called the worker's name and said, "Won't you please let me help you find employment in another place? You can use your medical training to save lives instead of taking them."

Unexpectedly, the woman turned to Judy and said, "Let me ask you a question. Do you think it is okay to euthanize dogs?"

Judy and I looked at each other incredulous that she asked such a thing. Before we could answer, the worker said, "What's the difference?"

Imagine that! The abortion clinic worker actually equated aborting babies with euthanizing dogs. Judy's attempts to reach out to the workers and help them find employment in other healthcare facilities was often successful. Her greeting from the sidewalks to the abortion workers was respectful, but with a generous degree of conviction. I've wondered how the workers could walk away from her kindness.

I am confident that one day abortion-on-demand will no longer be legal in America. Doesn't history demonstrate that eventually insanity and madness gives way to saneness and civility? If not, then no society would be left on the planet. Those promoting genocide would have completed their jobs long ago. The American Holocaust, too, will one day be a thing of the past.

When it ends, one can be assured our children and grandchildren will seek answers to those foreboding questions that are certain to be asked: *"Father, Mother, what did you do to stop the killing of the innocents?" "Grandfather, Grandmother, what did you do to save the babies?"*

How will we answer them? This is the challenge Judy lays before us in this book.

I understand that a foreword to a book is largely a recommendation of the author's qualifications. I assure you that Judy Madsen Johnson is duly qualified for many reasons. Here are two:

Foremost is her love for and commitment to her Savior. Judy's faithfulness as a follower of Jesus Christ is evident to all who know her.

Judy is able to view people, born and pre-born, as those Christ treasures.

My prayer for you, the reader, is that as you delve into the following pages, you will discover the unsearchable riches of our Savior and His love for humanity and be compelled to stand with Him and others He has called into the pro-life effort.

Pastor Warren Fox
Bainbridge, Georgia

Introduction

"Plastic okay?" the checker asked."

I nodded.

He pointed to photos on the back of the register. "Would you like to give…"

Hesitating for a moment, I thought, *It's the annual March of Dimes Drive, and I must educate this man that healthy pre-born babies each year are left blind, or have some other "birth defect." 15,000 are miscarried each year as a result of their mothers having had this amniocentesis test.*

Instead, I saw it was another charity and responded, "That's a great cause, but I give to save babies from abortion. They are most on my heart."

"Yes, ma'am. But in some cases, it's better, you know, to keep them from pain and suffering. They're better off with Him," he said, looking heavenward.

"We'd all be better off with Him, but to kill a baby without her ever even taking her first breath?"

The poor man was like so many other Americans fed on the lies in the media, public discourse, and sadly, also from many Christian pulpits. Of course, he was ignorant that his race is now just twelve percent of the population. Black girls and women obtain one third of the abortions, fifty to sixty percent choose abortion. Is it an economic necessity? No, it's a "right" foisted on many by leaders in their own community.

This is not a black issue. Not a white issue. We are engulfed in our own moral malaise of doing what is convenient and self-serving, not stepping on another's toes. When votes must be taken to ascertain what marriage is, are we not on an epic slide into the eager arms of the enemy? Christians, too, have lost their way.

But not all. A remnant of soldiers, Christian and committed, peaceful and non-violent, are on the battle lines each and every day, fighting for Life. They will not give up. With an impassioned vitality, they persevere, pray, and hope reinforcements are on the way.

These are their stories. Be touched. Be proud.

Heroes and heroines still exist, calling us to join them.

Though voices of the fifty-six million have been silenced, please hear their cries.

CHAPTER 1

Roe v. Wade and the American Holocaust
Judy Madsen Johnson

Most Americans could not tell you that the U. S. Supreme Court Decision in *Roe v. Wade* made abortion legal at every stage of the unborn baby's development, not just before viability. How important is the ruling to the Church? You decide.

One baby has been killed by abortion every twenty seconds in America since January 22, 1973. A number greater than fifty-six million is too enormous for the human mind to grasp. Yet, this number is less by far because there is no way to track babies destroyed by abortion-inducing pills, including some birth control pills. And now "morning-after pills" are sold over the counter, even to minors.

Imagine a fire siren going off three times a minute, 180 times an hour, nonstop for forty years. You better believe you would notice. The reality, a deafening silence for years, has encompassed our society as though it were in a vacuum. Where's our heart-wrenching sorrow? Where's our prostration before Almighty God? Where's our Church?

Think ten times the number of those murdered in the Nazi Holocaust! Euphemistically, it's called *choice,* but truly, it *is* the American Holocaust.

Just as the Nazi government used propaganda to brain wash people's attitudes about the Jews, our own government through the Institute of Medicine has essentially declared that a woman's fertility is

1

an unnatural condition and a disease to be eradicated. Other "studies" have made unfounded assertions that the fetus is a parasite.

Human lives conceived in the image of God have been considered inconvenient, unwanted, or even despised by those who have preferred their untimely death. The feminist movement sold lies disguised as truth. Some women have claimed "empowerment over their bodies" as though they had inherited a vault filled with gold.

In this "One nation, under God," our *Ship of State* was set morally adrift by nine men robed in black. Though the U. S. Supreme Court could not define "when life begins," they passed judgment on the most vulnerable of society's members and our country has been in a culture-of-death free-fall ever since.

Roe v. Wade and the history which preceded it is condensed below. It will help explain this gross injustice perpetrated upon the tiny person in the womb:

In June 1969, Norma L. McCorvey, pregnant with her third child, returned to Dallas, Texas, where friends advised her to assert she'd been raped. Though abortion was illegal at the time, Texas law contained the rape and incest exception. However, there was no police documentation of the alleged rape, and her effort failed. McCorvey tried to arrange an illegal abortion, but the center had been shut down by law enforcement. Eventually, she was referred to attorneys Linda Coffee and Sarah Weddington, who were looking for the right pawn to advance "women's rights." They gave the plaintiff an alias, *Jane Roe*. McCorvey gave birth long before the case was decided as it was tied up in the courts for three years. Decades later she petitioned the U.S. Supreme Court to overturn the decision because it had been based on a false premise—she admitted the lies. They have refused her case.

The following text concerning the 1973 *Roe* Decision is copied with permission of the Liberty Counsel and has been lifted from its argument in the Alabama Supreme Court case of *Hope Elisabeth Ankrom and Amanda Helaine Borden Kimbrough v. the State of Alabama:*

The *Roe* court concluded that an unborn child was not a "person" guaranteed the right to life under the 14th Amendment. *Roe v. Wade*, 410 U.S. 113, 158 (1973). At most, the unborn child becomes "potential life" subject to protection by the state at "viability." *Id.* at 163. Consequently, women can "terminate" their pregnancy, *i.e.,* kill their unborn "non-viable" child, without interference from the state. As Professor Byrn

2

observed, as a result of *Roe* and the companion decision in *Doe v. Bolton*, 410 U.S. 179 (1973), unborn children can legally be denied the right to life until birth.71

...the *Wade* decision means at a minimum: that an unborn child is neither a fourteenth amendment person nor a live human being at any stage of gestation; an unborn child has no right to live or to the law's protection at any stage of gestation; a state may not protect an unborn child from abortion until viability; after viability, a state may, if it chooses, protect the unborn child from abortion, but an exception must be made for an abortion necessary to preserve the life or health of the mother; and finally, health having been defined in *Doe v. Bolton* to include "all factors-physical, emotional, psychological, familial, and the woman's age-relevant to the well-being of the patient," it follows that a physician may with impunity equate the unwantedness of a pregnancy with a danger to the pregnant woman's health-emotional, psychological or otherwise. Thus, even after viability, there is little that a state can do to protect the unborn child.72

The *Roe* Court based its sweeping reversal of centuries of legal and social protection of unborn children by focusing upon what it perceived as a lessening of recognition of the humanity of the pre-born child.73 That perception was, in turn, based upon societal changes that undermined the child-protective worldview prevalent immediately before and after World War II.74 71 72

"Byrn at 812-813."

"Political correctness" came into its own a few years later and by design, the pro-abortion advocates successfully manipulated the English language to further its agenda. Among some of the misleading rhetoric are the following common phrases:

- Abortion is an "interruption or termination of pregnancy" wherein the "product of conception" is disposed of.
- "A woman should make this decision after consulting her doctor or her god." (The father has no rights where the baby is concerned.)
- "Men want to keep women home; barefoot and pregnant."
- Couples (married or not) should consult family planning centers, especially Planned Parenthood to "determine the size and spacing of their family."
- "An abortion is safer than carrying a baby to term," stated in recent so-called studies by the Institute of Medicine.

3

- "Adoption is not an answer. You will always worry about whether your child is being fed, has clothes to wear, and if it is being abused."
- And finally—the biggie from Planned Parenthood—"babies are loud, smelly, and expensive, unless you want one."

CHAPTER 2

A Conversation that Helped Win an Election
Dr Jack Willke

At the 1980 Republican National Convention, Ronald Reagan chose George H.W. Bush as his vice-president. That immediately presented a problem.

Dr. Jack Willke had just been elected president of the National Right to Life Committee, NRTL. He very much wanted to have his organization support Reagan, but now it was complicated because Bush, Reagan's running mate, seemed to be pro-abortion. Jack decided to see what he could do about that.

On the last day of the convention, he took an elevator in the Pontchartrain Hotel up to the fourteenth floor, the convention headquarters. Jack explained who he was and said he would like to talk to Mr. Bush. The young lady answering the door seemed somewhat taken aback as Jack explained that it was important for the upcoming election.

"Would you please wait?" she asked.

A few minutes later she returned and said, "Mr. Casey will be seeing you." *Who was Bill Casey?* He was to become head of the Central Intelligence Agency. They sat and talked for a bit. Mr. Casey seemed quite sympathetic to NRTL's issue, and said he would arrange for Jack to meet Mr. Bush.

After about a thirty-minute wait, Jack was ushered into what obviously had been a smoke-filled committee meeting room. Mr. Bush got up from his chair, came over, and shook Jack's hand. They sat alone in the room.

Jack explained who he was, and his pro-life position. NRTL wanted to support the ticket, because Ronald Reagan was pro-life, but there seemed to be some doubt about Bush's position on the issue.

Jack Willke plainly told Mr. Bush that due to his uncertainty, he didn't know whether pro-life people would support the ticket.

Mr. Bush thanked Jack for his straightforward comment. "Let me tell you where I stand."

Jack held up his hand, interrupted, and said, "Please don't. I think perhaps if I could brief you on the entire issue, and you could think it over, I might possibly change some of your thinking."

"I know you've had some pro-life pickets shout at you, but these folks are not the heart of the movement. May I give you a professional briefing?"

Mr. Bush relaxed, sat back, smiled, and said, "I think that's a good idea, Doctor."

He fished for his business card and said, "We're taking some time off now, but when we get back to Washington, call up. I'll have (--- ----- ---------) set you up with an appointment."

Jack said, "I would like to be very respectful, sir, but that won't be sufficient."

"Oh?" Mr. Bush was surprised.

"To do this right would take the better part of three or four hours. That is what I'd like to request from you."

He almost swallowed his teeth, "Four hours?"

Jack interrupted, "Of course, I would like to change your opinion and make you pro-life. I may not do that, but if I can report in our *National Right to Life News* that you were so interested in this issue and so respectful of it that you gave me this kind of time, that will make a profound impression on our people."

Bush sat back, mulling this over for a bit. Then he said, "You're pretty convincing."

"I hope so."

6

He paused again, then said, "Okay uh—look, I am going back to Kennebunkport, our home in Maine, *umm* - let me carve out a time up there, and we'll set you up there for a morning. Will you come alone?"

"I'll probably bring one lady with me."

"That's fine," Bush said, "I will have one of my aides with me. We will meet at my home."

"Fine, Mr. Bush, we'll meet in the morning. My presentation will be medical and scientific with moral overtones. Would you mind if, perhaps after lunch, I could bring a few more political people with me? We can discuss the campaign."

Another pause and he said, "All right, let's do it. Here is the person to call."

Several weeks later, Jack entered the Bush home with his Political Action Committee director, Sandra Faucher, and his Kodak carousel projector.

The house, on a small peninsula, on a bit of a rise, extends into the ocean. A gentle ocean breeze wafted through the French doors. Bringing iced tea and snacks, Barbara Bush was a gracious hostess.

Jack set his projector on a small table. He and Mr. Bush sat on opposite sides. The aide provided a screen, and the briefing began. For about three hours Jack spoke, flipped on a slide, and spoke some more. Mr. Bush questioned and Jack answered. Occasionally, his aide spoke, as did Sandy, but basically it was a dialogue between Willke and Bush.

Barbara Bush sat about a dozen feet away, knitting. She spoke only once, "Well, what if the life of the mother is in danger?" Jack responded, and satisfied, she continued knitting.

Other pro-life leaders joined them for lunch. For two more hours they discussed the campaign.

When it was time to go, Jack said, "Well Mr. Bush, in Detroit you offered to give me your stand on pro-life. Now would you be so kind as to answer?"

He smiled, and looked at Jack with an *okay-you-did-it* sort-of look. He said, "I wasn't here before, but now I will support an amendment to the Constitution to forbid abortion and overturn *Roe v. Wade*, It will have to be a states' rights amendment, not a federal amendment."

Jack thought, *That is not where you were when I walked in the door this morning, was it?* Though Jack remained silent, he was grateful for Bush's changed position.

"When we publicized this news, the pro-life movement strongly supported the Reagan-Bush ticket, and the rest is history. "

For the purpose of this book, the Willkes contributed the above interesting episode.

Dr. and Mrs. Willke have been active in the pro-life movement for half a century. In April of 2013, Mrs. Barbara Willke passed away. An author of ten books, the Willkes' materials have been published in thirty-two languages. Dr. Jack Willke, M.D., is President of Life Issues Institute, and former President of the National right to Life Committee.

Contact: Dr. Jack Willke
Life Issues Institute
1821 W. Galbraith Rd.
Cincinnati, OH 45230
www.lifeissues.org
info@lifeissues.org

CHAPTER 3

Godfather of the Pro-Life Movement
Joseph Scheidler

In 1973 when the United States Supreme Court handed down its *Roe v. Wade* decision, striking all state laws against abortion and removing any protection for the unborn, Joseph Scheidler had a revelation. "I figured it was my vocation to use what I had studied to fight abortion."

His determination over the years has earned him the reputation, "Godfather of the Pro-Life Movement."

Joe earned a degree in journalism and public speaking from the University of Notre Dame and pursued what he believed was his vocation – the priesthood. Eight years he studied at St. Meinrad Benedictine Seminary, four as a monk in solitude, silence, and obedience. Philosophy and theology were his disciplines; he reveled in Gregorian Chant.

As his ordination drew closer, Joe realized the priesthood was not for him. Unsure of his path, he taught journalism and theology at Notre Dame and later at Mundelein College in Chicago. There, Joe met his wife Ann. She, their seven children and twenty-two grandchildren are happy he decided against the priesthood.

With a journalist's viewpoint, Joe deduced, "The obvious strategy was to keep his views about abortion on the front page of newspapers." He continually created ways to keep attention focused on abortion, and accepted each opportunity to speak at every venue.

9

The Fairness Doctrine, much talked about today on conservative talk radio, was repealed years ago, but in Scheidler's early pro-life work, the Fairness Doctrine required both sides of an issue be given equal time.

"Volunteers monitored TV, radio, and print news. Whenever they spotted a pro-abortion editorial, the pro-lifer immediately called the station or paper for rebuttal time. "The media had to give it to you," Joe recalls. Many talk shows scheduled debates on abortion because they recognized it was a flash point that attracted listeners.

People were inexorably drawn to the controversy—some out of curiosity—others, because they believed abortion was unconscionable. Some, because they wanted to keep abortion legal.

Joe found common ground among like-minded citizens, mostly Christian, in organizations like National Right to Life, Illinois Right to Life, and the National Committee for a Human Life Amendment. But Joe was more inclined to activism than other established pro-life organizations. During his college teaching days, he was involved in the Civil Rights Movement and had marched with Dr. Martin Luther King in the 1965 Selma-to-Birmingham, Alabama March. Joe believed the fight for the unborn needed a street presence as had the fight for civil rights.

Using the First Amendment rights guaranteed in the U. S. Constitution, Joe founded the Pro-Life Action League in 1980 to focus on activism.

Joe's journalistic background also taught him visual effects' value. "A picture is worth ten-thousand words," Joe reminds us. Just as William Wilberforce used graphic images of slave chains to change the hearts of his fellow Parliamentarians in Great Britain to end slave trade, Joe brings pictures of aborted babies to the public square.

"Americans need to see what abortion really is," says Joe. "The euphemism, 'pro-choice,' masks the truth about abortion. That 'choice' results in a dead baby. Every time."

In 1985, Joe wrote his book on activism, *CLOSED: 99 Ways to Stop Abortion*, collecting the various successful tactics he either used himself or heard from other pro-lifers. As he began to work with other activists around the country, they formed a coalition, known as the Pro-Life Action Network, PLAN. Their aim was to simultaneously carry out pro-life activities in various parts of the country.

Although never fully realized, PLAN's concept put the fear of God in the pro-abortion camp. Between Joe's aggressive style, his book

CLOSED, and appearance of a "conspiracy," the National Organization for Women slapped Joe with a lawsuit filed in 1986. Originally an anti-trust suit, NOW expanded it into a RICO (Racketeer Influenced and Corrupt Organizations) suit.

The *NOW v. Scheidler* RICO suit finally went to trial in 1998 after a U.S. Supreme Court unanimous ruling that the RICO statute could be used against protesters. Scheidler lost the case in the District Court and again in the Appellate Court. However, he was vindicated eight to one by the Supreme Court in 2003. NOW refused to accept the Supreme Court's ruling. They failed to reignite the case against Joe and lost again in 2006. Joseph Scheidler's unanimous victory was sweet, indeed.

NOW v. Scheidler isn't settled yet. Scheidler's costs incurred in the course of the trial have not been awarded. The case has been alive for twenty-eight years—which may be some sort of record. In the history of the federal courts, none other has gone to the Supreme Court three times.

Over the years while his lawyers dealt with the RICO case, Joe continued his aggressive pro-life battle. He recorded a three-minute radio Hotline nearly every day. He reported pro-life news, announced pickets and events, and offered his editorials on court rulings and local laws.

Featuring former abortion providers, the first of such assemblies, Joe held conferences, and produced two powerful videos from their testimonies, *Meet the Abortion Providers* and *Abortion: the Inside Story.* Due to increased publicity brought on by the RICO suit, both Joe's reputation and support grew, providing funding to complete a project he could not afford earlier. The training video on sidewalk counseling is one of Pro-Life Action League's signature missions. *No Greater Joy* was introduced in 2000 and has received rave reviews by pro-lifers who are anxious to learn how to effectively reach out to abortion-bound women at the abortion clinics.

Joe says he will never retire from the abortion battle. His son Eric has joined him on the streets and is coordinating nationwide pro-life activism. Even Joe's grandchildren are out on the streets and highways with him. The Scheidlers say they plan to keep standing until abortion is unthinkable.

Contact: Joseph M. Scheidler, National Director
Pro-Life Action League
6160 N. Cicero Avenue, Suite 600
Chicago IL 60646
Phone: 773-777-2900
E-mail: joe@prolifeaction.org

CHAPTER 4

Pastor to the Pre-born
Rev. Ed Martin

"Ending abortion is easy. Finding the Christians to do it is the hard part," Rev. Ed Martin, Pastor to the Pre-born, has frequently declared. It is his creed.

He emphasizes, "If we have enough Christians out on the street each time they kill children, abortions will drop dramatically."

A clinic director once told Ed, "When one person with a sign stands in front of my clinic on days we do the procedures, over thirty per cent of our clients never show up. When two dozen or more stand outside, over half cancel their appointments."

When Christians stand outside death's door, more babies survive.

Pastor Ed's commitment is driven by his deep love for Jesus. He knows Jesus loves these children and has a great plan for them. Ed goes to the abortion mills each day, serving his Savior. He believes that Jesus wants all his followers to stand for Life and help save these children.

Pastor Ed doesn't just tell people to come out to the mills, he leads by example. Most days, you'll find him at death's door, offering help and love to abortion-minded mothers. He has done this since 1982 and will not stop until the Lord takes him home.

He also takes the "Gospel of Life" to other communities. In the past thirty years he has visited every state but North Dakota to preach this message. Traveling abroad, his message has been heard in many countries where he's offered pro-lifers help to form and grow their own groups. Ed has appeared on many national and local TV and radio programs and been widely quoted in print media across America.

In the early nineteen eighties Ed co-founded Rescue America with Don Treshman. When Christians put their bodies between the abortionist and his victim (the unborn child), it's called "rescue." Rescue America organized rescues or sit-ins at abortion mills throughout America, Ireland, and Puerto Rico. During these demonstrations, police were summoned and frequently, Christians were arrested.

Pastor Ed participated in over a hundred rescues between 1986 and 2001. Two cases landed at the U. S. Supreme Court. The first was the Madsen Case where Ed Martin was a co-petitioner with Judy Madsen and Shirley Hobbs. The court-decreed injunction, otherwise known as a "bubble zone," prohibited free speech on the public sidewalk. Liberty Counsel argued before the Justices, and they ruled six-to-three against the petitioners. The bubble zone remained.

The second case was a RICO suit that found its way to the Supreme Court but was remanded to the first circuit court in Puerto Rico. RICO was never intended for pro-life disputes, rather, to prevent racketeering and guarantee protection against financial deception. This case seemed doomed for the defendants. The judge assigned to the case was an ardent pro-abortion advocate. When revealed that her lawyer husband defended pro-abortion clients, she recused herself. A fair and impartial judge dismissed the case.

Pastor Ed Martin has been sued in over nineteen suits including RICO, the Hobbs Act, the KKK Act and many local injunctions. With the help of God and good legal representation, Ed Martin has won all these cases.

One of the great honors of his ministry, Ed was once asked to lead the opening prayer at the annual National March for Life in Washington DC. Over 500,000 people attended. Millions more listened to the March for Life broadcast on Christian TV stations across America. After Ed prayed, then President George Bush addressed the enthusiastic throng.

In 2005, Ed took two and a half months away from the abortion mills to assist Randall Terry with his efforts to save Terri Schiavo from starvation by order of a lone judge. Although their efforts failed and Terri died a horrible death, pro-life efforts to stop cold-blooded murder evident in all types of euthanasia has accelerated.

To save babies, Ed has traveled millions of miles wearing out one second-hand van after another. After relocation to Jacksonville, the first year and a half, Ed stood alone at four abortion mills on alternating days. In four and a half years since Ed's vigil began in Jacksonville, abortions dropped from 8,600 per year to a fifteen-year low of 6,800 abortions. God's Spirit moved as a result of Ed's faithfulness, and thousands now stand beside Ed to save babies' lives from death.

Through the years, Pastor Ed has used special events to draw many more Christians to the death camps. He led the Forty Days for Life in Jacksonville twice yearly for three years. Between these campaigns, Ed headed the Family for Life, a group who pray and offer help to mothers every day that abortions are taking the lives of the unborn.

Family for Life hosts Jericho Marches, memorial services for the unborn, youth marches, and prayer and praise services. These events attract hundreds. A fresh fire of faith has filled many hearts with compassion for the babies.

Pastor Ed firmly believes the united Body of Christ can best fight this great evil. He encourages Christians of all beliefs to join together outside the death camps. When Christians set aside denominational differences and come together for a common cause—saving unborn children—Ed knows great things happen. Unity of the body of Christ is different than ecumenism in that every person keeps their deeply-held beliefs and simply loves and respects others as together they save children from death.

Pastor Ed Martin has been married to Linda, his wonderful wife and the love of his life for forty-five years. They have three sons and their wives, and three grandchildren.

Ed and Linda recently moved from Jacksonville, Florida to Conyers, Georgia in the Atlanta area. God's new assignment brings Pastor Ed to minister at some of Atlanta's death camps. The move will give them opportunities to enjoy and be blessed by their family while God still uses this seasoned veteran for Life!

Contact: Pastor Ed Martin
Conyers, GA
Phone: 904-214-4908
E-mail: prolifeminister@peoplepc.com

CHAPTER 5

Death to Life
Dr. Beverly McMillan

As a college sophomore, she was faced with a decision–would she continue to live according to values taught by her family and the Catholic Church?

Rampant secular humanism surrounded Beverly McMillan when she left home in 1960 at eighteen to start her pre-med studies at the University of Tennessee.

Attending Mass and Communion one last time, she told God *goodbye*. Her friends seemed more real than He did, but she added, "If you *are* real, I hope you come back and get me someday." Beverly boycotted church for fourteen years. Blinded to God's creative work, she convinced herself that the human body she studied had somehow evolved out of mud, a la Darwin.

After graduating in the top third of her medical class, Beverly completed an internship in Memphis and married an agnostic classmate. She went on to study Obstetrics and Gynecology at the Mayo Clinic in Rochester, Minnesota. Part of her training involved a six-month rotation at Cook County Hospital in Chicago. Six weeks of that time included an assignment to the "Infected Ob Ward." She admitted fifteen to twenty-five women each night from the back-alley abortion mills. The year was 1969, four years before *Roe v. Wade* legalized abortion. *What kind of butchers worked on these women?*

The following morning, she took each patient to a small treatment room. Without anesthesia, she performed D & C's to remove whatever infected tissue the abortionist left in the uterus. Compounding the indignity, nurses and physicians treated these women with great contempt. At the end of her six-week rotation, it seemed obvious to Beverly that legalizing abortion would improve women's lot both medically and emotionally.

Abortion was legalized in 1973 by the U. S. Supreme Court, in all fifty states for all nine months of pregnancy. Shocked, but exultant, Beverly, in her central Kentucky private practice, bought a suction machine and offered first-trimester abortions to her patients.

One year later, Beverly's husband finished his residency and moved their family of three little boys to Jackson, Mississippi. She opened her practice in January 1975 and began a difficult year, 600 miles from family and friends. Her solo practice was slow in building. Beverly missed having work to keep her mind occupied.

That spring she met a group of citizens and clergy who wanted a freestanding abortion clinic in Jackson. There were none in the entire state. She agreed to help the group and by fall, they opened Family Health Services, a first-trimester abortion facility.

In January 1976, Beverly assessed the past year and realized she had achieved virtually every worldly goal she had set— an apparently stable marriage, three healthy sons, a thriving private practice, a busy abortion service including several other physicians to share the workload, a nice house, and a new car. The irony—Beverly was depressed— miserable. Thoughts of suicide rang through her mind.

She found a self-help book, *The Power of Positive Thinking* which attracted her attention. The first chapter ended, instructing the reader to affirm ten times daily:

"I can do all things through Christ who strengthens me" Philippians 4:13 (21st Century King James). She thought, *What the heck, I'm desperate, I'll just say the thing!*

"When I coughed out, 'I can do all things through Christ who strengthens me,' Jesus Himself was suddenly there in the car with me. Not a vision, but palpably present, in the back seat, behind my right shoulder, emerging as the *Hound of Heaven*."*

---

* A poem by Francis Thompson (1859-1907) telling of God's pursuit after a lost soul.

This was utterly beyond anything in Beverly's past experience. "I probably repeated that verse one hundred times, full of an awesome joy."

At the end of the book, Dr. Peale instructed the reader to find Christian fellowship and read the Bible every day. Beverly began fellowshipping with a godly Protestant woman whom she met the previous summer. She confided in her friend about opening the abortion clinic. The friend secretly contacted one of her prayer partners; they covenanted to pray for Beverly. Within six months, she was a Child of the King.

Beverly also bought a Bible and read it, front to back. Her depression vanished. Strangely, she found it difficult going to the abortion clinic. One of her last abortions was a "teaching" performance.

The abortion-clinic secretary asked Beverly to show her what she did at the sink after each abortion. The technique entailed identifying all the parts – two arms, two legs, a spine, a skull, and the placenta. If some were missing, Beverly knew where they were. She would have to suction and scrape the uterus again; otherwise, her patients would wind up like the unfortunate women at Cook County.

"As I showed her the parts, I was suddenly arrested by the baby's arm. The twelve-week-old baby was a boy, and his perfect little biceps' muscle chilled my heart. An image of my youngest son proudly showing me his "big" arm muscle flashed before me. The thought, *What am I doing?* pierced me deeply. At that point, I completely lost my stomach for abortion."

Beverly resigned from the abortion clinic in 1978. Her marriage ended in divorce one year later, but she found strength to survive devastation through her Christian faith.

In 1983 she met and married Roy McMillan. Roy's soft heart for the unwanted, unborn babies had its roots in his personal history: Abandoned at birth in 1943 on the steps of a Baptist church in Alexandria, Louisiana, Roy is thankful abortion wasn't legal back then. By 1986 he was a full-time pro-life activist, organizing Operation Rescue sit-ins. His example challenged Beverly.

Dr. Beverly McMillan is immediate past-president of Pro-Life Mississippi, and has now retired from her Ob-gyn practice. She and Roy are active parishioners of St. Richard Catholic Church.

"God has been faithful to me in this spiritual journey. I am not haunted by the hundreds of children I aborted."

One of Beverly's favorite scriptures is, "*If we confess our sins, He is faithful and just to forgive us our sins, and to cleanse us from all iniquity*" 1 John 1:9, (Douay Rheims).

Contact: Beverly McMillan
beverly.mcmillan7@facebook.com

CHAPTER 6

Christian Soldier
Joan Andrews Bell

The story of St. Joan of Arc, the nineteen-year-old who rode out to lead France in war, has thrilled generations through the centuries. Wearing heavy armor, Joan hoisted her country's flag for all to see as she galloped to battle.

This French peasant girl, against all odds, recovered her homeland from the English. She claimed divine guidance, yet a Bishop tried her as a heretic. In a shocking act of treachery, Joan of Arc, the Maid of Orleans, was burned at the stake. Church hierarchy ignored her significant victories in the One-Hundred-Year War.

In many ways, Joan Andrews mirrors the image of St. Joan. She, too, saw injustice. Joan Andrews' passion burned against murder of innocent babies unable to defend themselves.

"I expected the uprising of the Catholic Church. That did not come." She went forth bravely to right those wrongs. Soft spoken, gentle, and deeply religious, Joan Andrews displayed great courage and boldness, virtues shared by Joan of Arc.

"She was in her early 20s when *Roe v. Wade* became national law, and Joan took that judicial decree almost as a personal affront. It is no exaggeration to say that the whole of her life since that day has been spent in aggressive, sustained opposition to it. Arrested nearly 200 times, Joan has been convicted of felony trespass fifty-seven times." *(Patrick Henry Reardon, Touchstone Archives.)*

Joan was engaged with the heartbreak of legalized abortion from the beginning, "I could not express my shock and horror in 1973 with the abortion decision. I made plans and preparations to disarm the killing weapons in the abortion centers and prayed for guidance and strength. In December 1973, I headed by bus to Chicago to begin this effort which I expected to become my life from that moment on until the holocaust ended, or God called me to leave this life."* *(You Reject Them, You Reject Me, The Prison Letters of Joan Andrews. Richard Cowden-Gujido.)*

In Pensacola, Florida, Joan finally attempted her plan. She successfully disabled the plug from a suction machine, and also made un-sterile the abortion utensils. No babies were killed in that abortion center for days afterwards. She was charged in March 1986 with "burglary, malicious mischief, resisting arrest, and assault." The latter charge carries a life sentence in Florida, but it was dropped when found to be false. Total fabrications are not uncommon toward peaceful, non-violent pro-lifers.

Joan was denied a jury trial, also common to those arrested on behalf of unborn babies, possibly because liberal judges fear the accused may be offered mercy by their peers.

Whether in the courtroom or prison, Joan determined that she would become passively noncompliant in solidarity with the unborn. Infuriated, the judge punished Joan by placing her in solitary confinement, denying her the right to attend Mass.

That same court day, two men convicted of accessory to murder were given four-year sentences. Joan, sentenced to five years in prison, was placed among Florida's most dangerous inmates in maximum security at Broward Correctional Institute in Miami.

The governor received over 20,000 letters asking her pardon, commutation, or clemency. Thousands of pro-lifers from Florida and other states joined in a huge Tallahassee rally and marched up the broad boulevard to the Capitol Building. After serving two and a half years of her excessive and punitive sentence, Joan received a pardon by then Governor of Florida, Robert Martinez, on October 15, 1988.

The late Chuck Colson said, "Joan Andrews is one of America's genuine heroines—a woman who puts her life on the line for her convictions."* (Inscription on book cover, *The Prison Letters of Joan Andrews.*)

Joan chose her conscience over civil laws that discriminated against the personhood of the unborn baby, unremitting in peaceful sit-ins to the present day.

Many would disapprove of Joan's breaking the law, but over 75,000 Americans have done likewise. Babies' lives have been saved when birthmothers change their minds. Doubtless thousands, now twenty-nine and younger, of those saved are having children of their own.

Mother Teresa of Calcutta wrote to Joan in prison: "You have offered all to God and accepted all suffering for the love of Him—because you know that whatever you do to the least or for the least, you do it to Jesus—because Jesus has clearly said, If you receive a little child in my name you receive Me. We are all praying for you. Do not be afraid. All this suffering is but the kiss of Jesus—a sign that you have come so close to Jesus on the cross—so that He can kiss you."

Faithfulness to her cause denied Joan a personal life, separation from her family, and of course, marriage. "As a girl, my dream was always to marry a wonderful, devout Catholic man and raise a huge family of barefoot kids (hopefully on a farm). But he never came."

After twenty years serving the Lord on the frontlines, Joan became Mrs. Christopher Bell. Now Joan is a mother to seven children, six of whom are adopted.

God took time to arrange just the right husband for Joan. Chris helps homeless pregnant women. He co-founded Good Counsel in 1985 with his spiritual advisor, Father Benedict Groeschel.

The Bells embrace each other's love for life and children, playing supporting roles to the other. In 1998, Joan served nearly three months for a Pittsburgh arrest. Chris took charge of the children at home.

When released early, Joan spent the night at a friend's home. The next morning she returned to the Allegheny County Court to testify on behalf of a pregnant woman, befriended in prison, who was at risk to miscarry. While incarcerated, Joan had arranged for her own lawyers to petition for a medical furlough for this woman.

"Throughout her jail stay, Joan helped arrange releases of a dozen such women, and persuaded one young inmate to cancel her abortion and give the baby for adoption. 'If for no other reason, being in jail was worth it just to save that one baby,' she told the *National Catholic Register*."

Contact: Christopher Bell
Good Counsel Homes, Inc.
PO Box 6068 Hoboken NJ 07030
Pregnant? Need Help 800-723-8331

CHAPTER 7

Nine Lives Against Abortion
Randall Terry

"It does not take a majority to prevail... but rather an irate, tireless minority, keen on setting brushfires of freedom in the minds of men." Samuel Adams' quote is one of Randall Terry's favorites.

Head and shoulders above many peers, Randall Terry's passion and focus to end legalized child killing has figuratively accorded him nine lives against abortion.

Randall has little fear or concern about naming the perpetrators. He draws attention to both those wanting to hide in the shadows and those who promote the grisly murder of the unborn. Always up to the task, willing to take risks, Randall is definitely one who will never disappoint as one looks to see the light of truth expose the evils of legalized child killing. The founder of Operation Rescue continues in his quest to end this American scourge and holocaust.

Operation Rescue was the brainchild of Randall Terry in 1986; he became active in his hometown of Binghamton, NY. Though relatively unknown, Randall nonetheless soon became prominent in the movement and built upon the legacy of people like John Ryan, John O'Keefe, and Joan Andrews Bell.

His signal achievement— what no one else had done before— was to mobilize thousands against the child killers. Randall called this movement Operation Rescue, (OR). From 1987 to 1994, OR became nationally prominent, and then the Clinton Administration, led by Attorney General Janet Reno, passed and used FACE (Freedom of

24

Access to Clinic Entrances) to deter the winning strategy of Operation Rescue. This was Randall's impact on the pro-life movement, and the lists below are the highlights of OR under its founder at its pinnacle:

- Took activism to a new level by drawing thousands in front of multiple abortuaries in several cities simultaneously.
- 75,000 arrests over the span of 1987-1993, the most ever recorded in national history for a non-violent movement.
- Opened forty-plus affiliate offices throughout the country.
- Linked the gospel and scriptures to action and mobilized the evangelical world to the movement.
- Changed the way law enforcement dealt with the large number of non-violent protestors.
- FACE law enacted as a direct result of OR strategies, changing national laws.
- Politicians held accountable for their pro-life stances. They feared rejection by this organization if wayward in their word.

A highlight of Randall Terry's career resulted in an over three-month incarceration at the Allenwood Prison Camp in Allenwood, PA. He had exposed then candidate Bill Clinton to an "appointment" with a late-term aborted fetus:

Randall and his group had publicly announced they were intent on showing a fetus to Mr. Clinton sometime during the Democratic National Convention. Upon hearing this plan on television, Judge Robert Ward, Federal District Court of New York City, issued from the bench a restraining order against Randall and others from coming within 500 feet of candidate Clinton.

Harley Belew was contacted and Randall ordered Mr. Belew not to ask questions, nor read the paper, nor listen to the news, in order to protect Mr. Belew from violating this injunction. Mr. Belew successfully obtained Mr. Clinton's autograph on a newspaper that covered the body of a dead baby. Upon moving the paper, this fetus was fully revealed to Mr. Clinton. Several cameras caught the unsuspecting Clinton's shocked expression as he looked abortion's horrific reality in the face, the very "choice" he supported.

Due to numerous lawsuits, primarily instigated by Planned Parenthood, Randall was forced to abandon OR. The FACE laws were successful at emasculating tactics utilized by OR that had worked so effectively for years.

This took a toll on his family as well, which culminated in a divorce from his first wife Cindy Dean in 2000, the cause of much personal as well as public pain. In many instances, uncharitable comments and rejection from others in the pro-life movement were directed at Randall and his family. Since that time, he remarried, converted to Roman Catholicism, and continues to be outspoken in the pro-life arena.

In characteristic style, Randall Terry rebounded, and re-entered the pro-life arena by running for the United States Congress in Florida in 2005. During this time the family of Terri Schiavo recruited Randall Terry to bring about awareness of Ms. Shiavo's case, as it was virtually unknown at the time. Through his intervention, the plight of Terri Schiavo became indelibly etched in the consciousness of America, and set off a firestorm of ethical and moral discussions among the majority of Americans.

When the premier Catholic University in America, Notre Dame, tendered an invitation for the most pro-death American president in the nation's history, Barack Obama to give the commencement speech and receive an honorary Doctorate in Law, Randall directly confronted the Catholic hierarchy.

Randall instigated a protest so large that it garnered the spotlight of the international media for four days. Eighty-eight people were arrested and charged with criminal trespass. Despite the fact Randall had about twenty core people on his team, this event garnered more attention to the cause of legalized child killing than all of the other church-sponsored and private nonprofit 501 c 3 organizations combined.

Love him or hate him, one cannot help but be challenged to his core by the antics and activities of Randall Terry.

Like the quotes of days gone by, Randall Terry's is this, "In order to toss legalized child killing onto the ash heap of history, it will take direct confrontation of this nation's consciousness to accomplish the true goal of the pro-life movement—make illegal the murder of any child from conception to birth."

(Editor's note: Unlike the others whose stories are contained here, Randall Terry's article was written for him by a respected colleague, George Offerman. At the time of this writing, Randall Terry was a Democratic candidate for President of the United States. Terry's pro-life campaign, was waged across America as he opposed our incumbent President Barack Obama.)

Contact: Randall Terry
Society for Truth and Justice
PO Box 910
Romney WV 26757
Phone: 304-289-3700
www.voiceofresistance.org

CHAPTER 8

Unthinkable
Fr. Frank Pavone

Fr. Frank Pavone declares, "The goal of Priests for Life is not just to make abortion illegal. Our goal is to make abortion *undesirable, unavailable,* and *unnecessary* in the eyes of those who choose death, not life. Our goal is to make abortion *unthinkable!* Why is it so hard to reach that goal? If people take the time and trouble to look closely and carefully at the evil of abortion, they will not be able to live with themselves. Therein, lies the challenge.

We can pretend there is nothing that can be done, and end up either not engaged in the battle, or engaged in it as a *hobby,* something to be squeezed in when *more important* things don't demand our attention. And we never take on tasks that will either require too much sacrifice or prove wrong the misconception that we will fail.

Because there is pain....a pain shared by all in some way...the kind of pain when a person realizes, sometimes dimly, an evil is taking place in their midst. Similarly, that if they do something about it, there will be a price to pay. It will require a life change. How do they resolve the dilemma? Bury the issue? Tuck it away in a comfortable place in the mind and get on with life? Don't deal with something that can rock their very existence?

"If you say, 'But we knew nothing about this,' does not he who weighs the heart perceive it? Does not he who guards your life know it? Will he not repay each person according to what he has done?" Proverbs 24:12, (NIV).

"The task we face is to point out to our brothers and sisters that the price to be paid by ignoring this issue is greater than the price to be paid addressing it. We do that by connecting the issue to the other evils, ills, concerns they do hold close to their heart."

Many ills in our society proceed directly from abortion on demand. As an example, Fr. Pavone related student killings in schools to *Roe v. Wade*. "Children will stop killing children when parents stop killing children."

It is necessary to connect society's other besetting problems with the abortion experience. Resolution will not be achieved until abortion has been dealt with first.

Commenting on the biblical image of *the gates of hell*, Fr. Pavone pointed out, "a gate stands still, so who is storming the gates? It is the Church taking the initiative and storming the gates of hell. The gates of hell/death must flee in the presence of the Church, the people of life."

"And they shall fight against thee; but they shall not prevail against thee; for I am with thee, saith the Lord, to deliver thee" Jeremiah 1:19, (KJV).

If we plumb the depth of the horrific problem of abortion, and how entrenched it is in our society, there are two ways we might respond: dedication or fanaticism.

Total dedication, not fanaticism, is being willing to give one's life in the cause. Fanaticism means that, except for the one focus we have, our personality shuts down and we disconnect from reality.

The warrior soul, on the other hand, devotes all of his fully-functioning personality to the cause. It is precisely because he is connected to reality that he sees that cause as all-important.

General George S. Patton, Jr., in his 1926 essay, "The Secret of Victory," wrote, "The secret of victory lies not wholly in knowledge. It lurks invisible in that vitalizing spark, intangible, yet as evident as the lightning—the warrior soul. The fixed determination to acquire the warrior soul, and having acquired it to either conquer or perish with honor, is the secret of victory."

Father Pavone continues his narrative about warrior souls...those who would make abortion unthinkable. "I cannot count how many warrior souls I've met across the country in the pro-life movement:

- An elderly woman who could not walk, yet confined to a wheelchair and battling cancer, insisted on going regularly to the abortion mill to join others praying on the sidewalk to save children about to be killed.
- Young people who relocate to unfamiliar parts of the country and, for little or no salary, undertake full-time pro-life work that brings them ridicule even from those they thought were friends. Yet nothing matters more to them than stopping the killing.
- A pastor who told his people that if they didn't like his preaching on abortion, they could go elsewhere, but he would be working to help all his brother priests preach this message. There would be no parish where it wasn't heard.
- Men and women in the media who challenge their colleagues to present the truth about abortion. They don't care that their colleagues ridicule them or that they may lose opportunities to advance up the company ladder. What matters most is the victory for truth."

Social change doesn't come through committees and boards. It comes through warrior souls. It's something like what scripture tells us:

"This is how we know what love is: Jesus Christ laid down his life for us. And we ought to lay down our lives for our brothers" 1 John 3:16, (NIV).

The above chapter is taken from two of Fr. Pavone's messages.

FR. FRANK PAVONE, ordained in 1988, serves in the Amarillo Diocese full-time in pro-life leadership with his bishop's permission. Fr. Pavone is National Director of Priests for Life, President of the National Pro-life Religious Council, and National Pastoral Director of the Silent No More Awareness Campaign and Rachel's Vineyard, the world's largest post-abortive healing ministry. He averages preaching-and-teaching visits to four states weekly. He produces programs for religious and secular radio and television. Mother Theresa had him speak on life issues in India. He's addressed the Pro-Life Caucus of the U.S. House. Vatican-appointed to the Pontifical Council for the Family and Academy for Life. He was at Terri Schiavo's bedside as she lay dying. Fr. Pavone has won numerous pro-life awards and honorary doctorates, and is an author of two books.

Contact: Fr. Frank Pavone
Priests for Life
PO Box 141172
Staten Island, NY 10314
Phone: 718.980.4400, x 224
www.priestsforlife.org

CHAPTER 9

Blood Money
Carol Everett

The death of one woman, the maiming of nineteen others to the point of major surgery, all were encompassed in 35,000 abortions over six years. The following story, adapted from *The Scarlet Lady*, is told about one of the nineteen:

Jenni was beautiful—tall, model-thin with brunette hair. At twenty-one, she loved attention and knew how to get it—with her body. That was obvious the moment she danced into the clinic on a Wednesday afternoon.

I took her back to the examining room to be sized by a doctor before she paid for the procedure. "Take your clothes off from the waist down and have a seat on the edge of the table," I directed.

The doctor came in, patted Jenni on the leg and said with a reassuring smile, "Hi, baby. we're just going to check to see how big you are. It won't hurt."

"It looks like you're twenty-two weeks," the doctor commented as he finished the examination. "The pelvis is normal, so the procedure can be done without any problem. The fee will be seven hundred and fifty dollars if we put you to sleep, and it will be easier on you if we do. Do you have the money?"

"Yes, and I have enough to be put to sleep—seven hundred and fifty dollars. Connie said it is much easier if I can afford to be put to sleep. I hate pain. I have a fifteen-month-old daughter living with my parents. Her birth nearly killed me. I just can't stand pain," Jenni spoke quickly. Her voice sounded young and carefree.

"Let's go up to the front desk, so you can pay."

I went to check the operating room to be sure it was ready. The instruments had to be prepared—large dilators, sterilized yet cool enough; a #16 cannula, a tube to insert into the uterus; and Bierhoff forceps, to remove the pieces of that pesky baby.

It took some time to get everything ready. I checked on Jenni several times, to make sure she was okay, that she wasn't getting too nervous.

Instinctively, I knew she had run away from problems back in Nevada. We discussed her leaving her daughter with her parents. Jenni didn't seem to miss her. It was as though the child was a part of her history, not a part of her life. She talked about several of her lovers, but never mentioned the father of the child.

"Jenni, everything is ready now," I called. "This won't take long."

After the anesthetist put her to sleep, I placed my hand on Jenni's abdomen. I felt movement, one of the only babies I can ever remember feeling move inside the mother during an abortion.

The doctor proceeded as normal. He cleaned the cervix with Betadine, dilated the cervix, and suctioned briefly to break the bag of amniotic fluid surrounding the baby. The baby did not move again after the doctor started suctioning. The next step required him to crush the baby inside Jenni's uterus and remove the baby piece by piece using Bierhoff forceps.

The first time the doctor reached in, he pulled out placenta. When he reached in the second time, he pulled out the lining around the colon. I saw the shock on his face. His ashen look told me it was serious.

Barely above a whisper, he spoke, "It's over. I pulled out omentum." Frantically, he tried to push the bowel back into the uterine cavity, but to no avail. "We have to take her to the hospital."

Another cover up. No press. No reporters. No lawsuit. None of the clinic employees really knew what happened to Jenni. She recovered, but oh what lies and deception, and sin stains on my soul.

Concerning abortion, Carol Everett was both a consumer and a provider. Carol's abortion, February 19, 1973, left a hole in her heart and her life. Nothing worked to fill the hole, but selling abortions to other women seemed the answer. She discovered the potential income hidden in the abortion industry behind words like *choice* and *privacy*. With a commission of twenty-five dollars per abortion, Carol only needed to *sell* 40,000 abortions a year to produce a personal income of $1,000,000. The business model called for three to five abortions a year from every girl they could reach between the ages of thirteen and eighteen. Abortions were sold through "how-to sex education" using low-dose birth control pills and defective condoms to lure innocent teens into sexual activity.

Carol's plan was in place with her goal in sight when an encounter with the living Lord Jesus Christ turned her life around. She began to pray.

It was not long before the clinic was caught by a television reporter's investigation, performing abortions on women who were not pregnant. It was clear God had answered her prayers. He did not want her killing babies.

Since 1985, Carol has been actively involved in educating pro-lifers and supporting pregnancy-resource centers. The Heidi Group, named for Carol's aborted child, was founded out of her pain of abortion with two objectives:

- Educate and protect girls and women in unplanned pregnancies from the destructive choice of abortion.

- Offer hope and healing to abortion survivors, both women and men, and lead them to lives of freedom in Christ Jesus.

Carol and The Heidi Group pray the Lord will use their work to save millions of babies' lives physically and mothers' lives eternally. That is the goal of their strategic planning and fundraising assistance.

In *The Scarlet Lady*, Carol dedicated her book as follows: "And to my unborn daughter, Heidi, and all the unborn who face her fate unless their cries, *Let me live! Let me live!* are heard.

As a non-profit, The Heidi Group's life-affirming work takes on many forms: education, conferences, intervening in unplanned pregnancies, and offering healing and hope to the survivors of abortion.

Carol Everett is the author of *THE SCARLET LADY; Confessions of a Successful Abortionist* and the reprinting titled, *Blood Money: Getting Rich Off a Woman's Right to Choose.*

Contact: The Heidi Group
Phone: 512-255-2088
www.heidigroup.org

CHAPTER 10

$100,000 Sermon
Pastor Johnny Hunter

Jail was seen as a small price to pay to save babies' lives. If mothers cancelled their abortion appointment because people sat or lay between them and the clinic, some would decide to keep their babies.

The year was 1992. Dr. Johnny Hunter served as Chairman of the Western New York Clergy Council in Buffalo, NY. He was already a pro-life leader and had participated in "rescues" across the country. Rescuers were willing to go to jail to save the life of a child by practicing non-violent civil disobedience. Rescuers blocked doors or driveways preventing abortions at a given place on a given day. Christians answered the call to biblical obedience, sacrificing their lives for *the least of these*.

Early in the rescue movement, before 1990, twenty-five people could shut down abortion for a day.

The cost of sacrifice increased as time passed. Christians from all walks of life, including prayer warriors and sidewalk counselors, were arrested. Prayer warriors who had not risked arrest—but prayed across the street for those who did—were also taken to jail. Occasionally, sidewalk counselors were arrested, illegally.

As the rescue movement rapidly became more effective in larger cities like Atlanta, Washington, DC, and New York City, the police response, with the help of Attorney General Janet Reno, intensified. Hundreds were arrested in a single day.

The Executive Branch of Government and the Federal Courts were determined to crush the Rescue Movement. A so-called "conspiracy theory" had emerged.

Dr. Johnny Hunter was threatened by a federal judge with a huge civil fine the first night he spoke at New Covenant Church in Buffalo. The judge ruled a certain scripture could not be read or quoted from the pulpit. An attorney sent by the judge reached Hunter before he went into the pulpit. "Pastor Hunter must not quote Proverbs 24:11-12:"

> *"Rescue those being led away to death; hold back those staggering toward slaughter. If you say, 'But we knew nothing about this,' does not he who guards your life know it? Will he not repay each person according to what he has done?"* (NIV)

Mentioned once, the fine would be $10,000. If repeated, the fine would double the previous fine and total $30,000, etc. That was the very verse the Holy Spirit had given Pastor Hunter. He wondered, *how many preachers would preach a sermon that could cost them a hundred thousand dollars?*

When Johnny Hunter told the attorney he intended to preach from that scripture, the attorney joyfully offered to represent him *pro bono* (for free). Rev. Paul Schenck, a Christian activist, introduced Hunter and informed the large crowd of the judge's ruling. Schenck then read the scripture several times and the people rejoiced.

As Johnny Hunter walked into the pulpit, a gubernatorial candidate jumped on stage and read the scripture also. Hunter quoted the scripture so often that night that it rang in everyone's ears.

The proverbial "heaping coals" upon the judge caused even more aggressive tactics in their prosecutions of pro-lifers, through all levels of law enforcement.

The rescues continued. It was Johnny Hunter's call to select the abortion site where Christians would go. No matter his decision, he cried for both the babies who were saved, and those who died. Not all clinics could be covered.

The Lord gave Hunter a vision for an event called, "The Spring of Life." Though the date had not been announced, pro-abortionists knew it was coming and obtained court injunctions against certain leaders. They overlooked Johnny Hunter. The goal to shut down a certain abortion site for two weeks occurred during Easter break. Nationally, pro-lifers responded as well as abortion radicals and homosexual groups in opposition.

Over 2,000 people risked arrest; half were jailed. Within the first few days, men and women were held in an armory, secretly converted with cages into a prison. Christians housed out-of-towners. Strangers became friends. Churches of various denominations worked together to feed the participants. Pastor Hunter's wife Pat handled daycare and teachers volunteered to teach the older children.

Doctors offered free pre-natal care and follow-ups for every mother who decided to keep her child. Lawyers formed a group, "Lawyers for Life," and represented every individual *pro bono*. Legal scholars such as John Broderick, famous "rescue attorney," stepped in to help. The American Center for Law and Justice was present and available.

None of that benefitted Johnny Hunter. Held for nine days without being charged, an attempt to bail him out was unsuccessful. Technically, he had not been charged. Amnesty International, a strange bedfellow, then stepped in and got him released.

Severe injustice—the personal testimonies of those involved would fill volumes. The punishment did not fit the "crimes." One pastor who had no involvement in the planning was sent to prison as co-conspirator. Putting up no defense, he took the legal hit so another pastor could offer leadership to other national rescues.

During a public press conference, Mayor of Buffalo, Jimmy Griffith (now deceased) welcomed the rescuers to the city. He stated, If you break the law, you will be arrested, but if one life is saved, it will be worth it!"

At a Christmas celebration that year, a young mother, Rose, came forward to place her baby, saved during the Spring of Life into the arms of the mayor. Tears rolled down his cheeks.

The rescuers have aged now and some are asleep. Many Americans did hard time in jails and prisons. Not seeking to risk arrest, however, they willingly encouraged others, put self aside, and followed Christ.

Pastor Dr. Johnny Hunter, an African American, now leads the cause to expose black genocide as instituted by the late Margaret Sanger, Founder of Planned Parenthood. With over one-third of abortions killing black babies, abortion is a racial disaster. As National Director of Life

Education And Resource Network (L.E.A.R.N.), Hunter is awakening the black church and community to the holocaust of abortion.

> Contact: Dr. Johnny Hunter
> P.O. Box 9400
> Fayetteville, NC 28311
> Phone: 910-868-5327
> jmhlearn@earthlink.net

CHAPTER 11

Aborted But Survived
Carrie Fischer

Wonder what a miracle looks like? Just look at Carrie Fischer. Abortion almost claimed Carrie's life when her mother aborted her forty-five years ago!

Why would a person want to do such a thing? Shirley already had two older children when she dated Carrie's birth father. When she realized she was pregnant and shared the news with him, he declared he wanted nothing to do with the baby. Their relationship walked out the door.

Devastated—she felt hopeless, abandoned—she thought abortion was her only option. Shirley went to a clinic, and the doctor performed an abortion procedure. It all seemed routine, but her abortion failed—she was still pregnant and perplexed. On June 10th, 1969, Carrie Holland was born. By God's grace, she had survived!

As a little girl, Carrie had recurring dreams of a baby in the womb fighting for her life. She remembers it distinctly, "I heard the cries and screams of this baby, and it frightened me. I had no idea that baby was me." The dream pattern continued for several years.

Until Carrie reached her teens, the failed abortion attempt was kept secret. Finally, Carrie's grandmother explained that Shirley had tried to kill Carrie. Because her birth father refused to be a dad, Shirley feared raising another child alone. It was confusing, mind-numbing to Carrie. *What was her grandmother talking about?*

"Why would my own mother want me killed? I found the courage to ask her, and Mom started crying. She confessed her regret and shame. My anger melted away as time softened my feelings.

Carrie's abortion left her with a facial disfigurement. Doctors predicted she wouldn't be normal; there would be mental retardation. Society labeled her as ugly and unacceptable. What a double blow to Shirley as she was already dealing with her own guilt.

School was a horrible experience…anyone's worst nightmare. Children taunted Carrie all during school; many of her teachers did also. She felt she was a nobody who didn't matter. Bluntly told she'd never have a normal life, a job, a date, or get married and have a family, Carrie thought, *I may as well just give up on any dreams. I'll never be much of anything anyway.* Those lies became Carrie's identity.

"I was bitter and angry. I hated life and I blamed God for all my pain and hurt."

In her thirties, Carrie attempted suicide. She swallowed a bottle of anti-depressants with a full bottle of wine. She lay down hoping not to awaken, but God intervened. Twice He gave Carrie back her life.

Carrie relates, "Amazingly, I woke up the next morning as usual, with absolutely no ill effects from the pills and alcohol. Then I realized God had a destiny and purpose for my life. I discovered my worth in Christ. He gave me self-confidence. I could now say and believe, even with the facial deformity, 'I am wonderfully beautiful. I truly love me.'"

"No longer did the lies I'd been told so often have power over me. I was healed, set free from my painful past. By God's mercy and grace, I forgave my birth mother. God changed her heart, too. She has always been there for me."

Carrie lived with her mother, who protected and provided for her the first forty-two years of her life.

God began turning many of Carrie's dreams into reality." On June 9, 2011, the day before her forty-second birthday, Carrie received a facebook message from a man named Richard Fischer. Weeks before, when Richard saw Carrie's profile picture, God spoke to him through the scriptures. He was deeply moved as he meditated on the disfigurement of Jesus, beaten before His crucifixion.

> *"…He had no beauty or majesty to attract us to him, nothing in his appearance that we should desire him"* Isaiah 53: 2, (NIV).

41

"Richard saw my disfigured face on a mutual friend's pro-life ministry page, and felt compelled to speak to me. When Richard learned that in all my life, I'd never been asked for a date, he cancelled plans to attend a Christian event in Georgia. Instead, he came to Houston to meet me face to face."

They spoke together for several days via phone and facebook chat, and arranged a double date at a Japanese restaurant near Carrie's home in Houston seven days after the first contact. When their wonderful evening concluded, they were both convinced God had foreordained them to become husband and wife.

A month later, they met in Orlando, Florida, where Carrie spoke at a pro-life event. The following day, Richard formally asked Carrie to marry him—a made-in-heaven romance—and a happy ending.

Original plans were to wait a year, but God gave them almost identical visions the same day. The word received in those visions, "It's time," was confirmed through Richard's trusted friend. Richard and Carrie were married September 22, 2011.

Seven months later, at the combined age of ninety-five, the Fischers were expecting their first child. God answered their prayers. Hadn't He answered Abraham and Sarah's; Zechariah and Elizabeth's? Richard and Carrie were wondrously joyful.

"At six weeks, we saw our baby's heartbeat in our first ultrasound. But a month later, on my forty-third birthday, we were devastated. I miscarried our baby. I've come to grips with the fact that not only did God know the miscarriage was going to happen, but He will use it to help us reach out and minister to others."

Abortion leaves scars that can take years to heal. It took Carrie a long time to move beyond the hurt, anger, and pain of her mother's abortion, and it will take time to heal from the loss of their baby, Zion Benjamin Fischer.

They hope, that by sharing their story, lives can be saved, healed, and restored. Carrie Fischer is available for speaking engagements.

Contact: Carrie Fischer
Phone: 865-719-3406
Wonderfullybeautiful69@yahoo.com
http://facebook.com/wonderfullybeautiful

CHAPTER 12

Digging Deeper, Information that Indicts
Troy Newman

Cold cases, forensic lab work, records research, and undercover witnesses are the stuff from which dynamic television series are made. It's also at the core of one very effective Christian pro-life organization, Operation Rescue.

Operation Rescue's modus operandi was not always as it is today. National attention in the late eighties and early nineties focused on the effective and highly-charged rescues. Videos of protestors dragged away to jail was paraded on America's nightly news. Pulses and hearts were quickened as if struck by lightning. Abortion came into America's living rooms.

However, in 1994, Operation Rescue lacked focused national leadership and the movement began to wane. Pro-life sit-ins, once local misdemeanors, became Federal felonies under the Clinton Administration with the passage of the Freedom of Access to Clinic Entrances Act, otherwise known as FACE. Hundreds of Operation Rescue affiliates across the United States struggled to realign their mission. Most closed altogether.

Meanwhile, through innovative strategies, Troy Newman, second in command under Jeff West of Operation Rescue West, closed over two dozen abortion clinics in the Southern California area. But it was not without cost.

In 1997, Janet Reno's Department of Justice sued him under FACE. Planned Parenthood and other abortionists also sued Troy for his efforts to use legal means to focus the media's attention on the illegal acts of the abortion industry.

The lawsuits only solidified Troy Newman's resolve to use the legal system to close abortion clinics.

Troy left California and relocated in Wichita, Kansas, America's Heartland. Few realized that Wichita, relatively conservative in its values and core beliefs, harbored the most notorious abortionist in the U.S., Dr. George Tiller. People are prone to bestow nicknames, but "Tiller the Killer" was well deserved.

George Tiller advertised across America and abroad that he was a specialist in late-term abortions, "fetal demise," and indeed, killed pre-born babies up to and including their actual date of delivery. Pro-choice doctors, restrained by their own state's legislation or unwilling to perform these grisly procedures themselves, sent patients to the geographical center of the country.

An anti-abortionist's fatal bullet brought Tiller down in his own church one Sunday morning in 2009. Tiller's life had been spared on one previous occasion, but he used his near "martyrdom" at the time to rally support among the abortion industry. His association with the H.H.S. Secretary, Kathleen Sebelius, then Governor of Kansas, was friendly and symbiotic—dollars exchanged for her election campaigns—immunity in the courts on his behalf.

It was Cheryl Sullenger's complaint that prompted the Kansas Board of Healing Arts to issue an eleven-count petition of wrongdoing against Tiller months before his death that would have soon resulted in disciplinary action. Like Troy, Cheryl Sullenger, Senior Policy Adviser for Operation America, had relocated from California where they had worked together.

Today, Operation Rescue's national headquarters is located in a former abortion clinic that Troy bought and closed. The filthy clinic, rat and roach-infested, was completely renovated to serve as the launching platform for Operation Rescue's successful efforts to close abortion clinics nationwide. Troy's laser is now directed beyond Wichita toward vulnerable, exploitive abortion businesses which kill babies and endanger and maim their mothers. In 2013, the Kermit Gosnell murder trial was a major focus.

Troy Newman depends on pro-life volunteers as he continues to find new ways to challenge the abortion industry's stranglehold on politics and culture.

Operation Rescue worked to expose and call for criminal charges against an illegal late-term abortion ring operated by Stephen Chase Brigham that spanned two states. Four abortionists' medical licenses were suspended as a result of the public spotlight that Operation Rescue helped shine on this horrific, illegal abortion scheme.

Some of Operation Rescue's projects throughout the country have made headlines in recent weeks. Troy's work blew the lid off the secret illegal "telemed" abortion pill internet-distribution scheme in Iowa: The client has no physical contact by a doctor, but receives drugs after a "Skype" examination. The entire state has been rocked by the undercover work of Operation Rescue.

The abortion industry is right to fear the work of Operation Rescue. Since 1991, the number of abortion clinics in the United States has dwindled from 2,173 to under 700 today. Over two thirds of all abortion clinics have closed, and polls show public opinion swaying in favor of the pro-life position. The majority of clinic closures are due to the type of legal and public scrutiny brought by Operation Rescue. Their tactics are now being adopted by other organizations.

The National Organization for Women, the Fund for the Feminist Majority, Planned Parenthood, the Nation Abortion Federation, and the Center for Reproductive Rights have all referred to Newman's Operation Rescue organization as one of the biggest threats to abortion rights in America. Just as we are judged by the company we keep, one must be impressed by Troy's enemies.

Operation Rescue co-founder Rev. Patrick J. Mahoney, who heads the Christian Defense Coalition in Washington, D.C., gave praise that is not taken lightly, "We are all really proud of what he (Troy) has accomplished."

Troy's groundbreaking work has been featured in *Rolling Stone Magazine*, *The Los Angeles Times*, *The New York Times, The Chicago Tribune*, and CNN. Newman gives hundreds of interviews each year. Several quotes follow:

- "Relentless" -NARAL Pro-Choice America 06/28/09
- "Operation Rescue chief Troy Newman has aggressively–and successfully–sought to reduce access to abortion in the U.S." - *Chicago Tribune*, June 10, 2008
- "Plays hardball…" – *LA Times*

"When I think of the goal of ending abortion, one of the people who comes foremost to my mind is Troy Newman. … He is routing the enemy in many ways. I praise the Lord for what Troy and his collaborators have been able to accomplish!" Fr. Frank Pavone, National Director, Priests For Life.

Troy Newman and Operation Rescue will not rest until every abortion clinic has a sign which says, "Closed for business."

Contact: Troy Newman
Operation Rescue
PO Box 782888
Wichita KS 67278-2888
Office: 316-683-6790
Toll Free: 800-705-1175, Fax: 916-244-2636
www.operationrescue.org

CHAPTER 13

A Problem or a Baby?
Sandy Epperson

In the summer of 1986, a precious young friend came to Sandy Epperson in tears. Lisa* was pregnant—by someone she really disliked—a drug dealer. Since no relationship had developed, Lisa decided to keep her pregnancy from him. She wanted him out of her life.

She asked Sandy, "Is abortion the answer?"

Sandy had never faced this before; she had her doubts. Sandy was an adult Christian, married mother of two, with no idea what consequences abortion might hold, or if it was simply a routine procedure.

She asked Lisa to find out more about abortion. They headed down the treacherous path so many before them have trod.

Lisa reported back to Sandy after she made a few calls. She was told, "Based on how far pregnant you think you are, it's not yet a baby. If you hurry before the week is over, it will be O.K. to have an abortion."

Lisa asked them if it would hurt, and they replied, "For fifty dollars more, you can be sedated." The two women agreed it was best to hurry.

Girls filled the lobby of the abortion clinic. Most seemed relaxed and unconcerned …even laughing. Later Sandy thought, *if I felt we were doing nothing wrong, why was I so uncomfortable?*

---

* Not her real name.

47

While her young friend checked in, Sandy waited in the lobby. Lisa looked scared. Sandy wanted to comfort her, but she was not allowed in the back abortion rooms.

After what seemed hours, Lisa came into the lobby. They exited without words, anxious to leave this place behind.

Sandy asked, "How are you?" Lisa nodded, her face was pallid and drawn.

They went to lunch. Neither were hungry, and if either one had broken down and cried, their tears would have pooled around them.

Lisa stayed at Sandy's home for a few days, but the abortion wasn't discussed... until four years later. Denials can last for decades.

Several years later, Sandy allowed herself to dig up the memories. She began the process of learning about abortion and was deeply pained by the counsel she had given her friend. The basic fact that life begins at conception devastated her. Sandy didn't have to read a library of books for God to break her heart.

"And you will seek me and find me, when you search for me with all your heart" Jeremiah 29:13, (NIV).

Earlier, Sandy had not sought God's answer, because it seemed the answer was obvious. She just wanted Lisa's problem to *get fixed.*

Most troubling to Sandy were the thoughts she had had, *it was a problem and not a baby.* God's Word says differently:

"There is a way which seems right to man, but its end thereof is the way of death" Proverbs 14:12, (NIV).

God had more to teach Sandy—it was a long journey. She needed to understand why she found herself crying so much. Contrary to the rhetoric of those who advocate abortion, Sandy learned that women who have aborted their babies experience Post-Abortion Stress. Sandy was going through that herself.

In the meantime, a position to direct the Center for Pregnancy opened at the church where she was on staff. She applied and became the director. Sandy put to good use her ability to evangelize, learned in her former role. She combined sharing the Gospel of Jesus Christ with her passion to prevent other women from choosing abortion.

One of Sandy's first tasks was to go through a post-abortion Bible study already underway at the Center. Soon after her restoration,

Sandy knew God had called her to be an active part of the healing process for women and men in abortions' aftermath. Yes, many men also suffer grief and loss after an abortion.

"Once you were alienated from God and were enemies in your minds because of your evil behavior. But now he has reconciled you by Christ's physical body through death to present you holy in His sight, without blemish, and free from accusation" Colossians 1:21-22, (NIV).

As director of the center, Sandy never wanted someone to say, "I didn't know; I chose abortion. I wish someone had told me."

Reaching out with the message that God says *"No"* to abortion (and why) is critical. Sandy discovered her calling for those who have had an abortion, to find God's forgiveness and grace, and His unending love for them. Using material called "First Steps," written by the previous director, Sandy continued the support groups until her retirement in 2010.

From her own tragedy to grace, Sandy affirms one of the greatest lessons of her life, "Christ is a miracle God and walking with Him keeps life amazing."

Did she really retire? Sandy has recently become a part of a new ministry, mentoring mothers one-on-one for twelve weeks. Christ is a life changer.

Sandy suggests you ask yourselves, "What can I do? I can simply be available when someone, anyone, asks me if abortion is the answer to their problem, and I now know that God says, '*No*' to abortion."

If you choose to be more actively involved, find a pregnancy center near you to be trained and to be used by our Lord in the direction and healing of so many women who feel they are in a crisis.

During her tenure at Center for Pregnancy, a ministry of First Baptist Church, Orlando, FL, Sandy was sent to other states by the Southern Baptist Convention to set up pregnancy resource centers patterned after the successful model she served. She also was a part of the team effort when a beautiful multi-million-dollar facility was constructed to meet the growing needs of the minority community surrounding their campus.

Early in 2012, Sandy went on assignment to Beijing, China for Heartbeat International, where she put to use her life-changing counseling. One young Chinese mother decided not to abort her baby girl.

Contact: Center for Pregnancy
3125 Bruton Blvd., Suite B
Orlando, FL 32805
Phone: 407-514-4517

CHAPTER 14

Police Officer Arrested
Chet Gallagher

Child sacrifice from biblical times has been tied to godless worship.

"Each child being ripped from its mother's womb and sacrificed to demons is an abomination before God," says Chet Gallagher, "but it is not the unforgiveable sin. God forgives and heals. Families that were destroyed by this sin can become cleansed and, receiving restoration, can be used in a significant way."

He affirms, as many others in pro-life leadership, that abortion is not often a subject preached in America's pulpits. As an evangelist, his passion is to move the Church toward its moral responsibility into the political realm.

Chet states, "My primary role is to go into churches and talk with pastors and teachers—'not the hirelings'—real men and women who love the Lord, but feel a misplaced compassion. So deeply is it imbedded in their members, they are kept from being effective in teaching about abortion." In their silence, the sin sick remain unhealed.

Who is Chet Gallagher?

First, who was Chet Gallagher? A striking figure as a Las Vegas motorcycle cop with shiny boots, a veteran officer of twenty years. He reflected, "It was a great job and I loved it."

Christian and pro-life, Chet had recently read in his Bible, *"If you falter in times of trouble, how small is your strength! Rescue those*

51

being led away to death; hold back those staggering toward slaughter" Proverbs 24: 10-11, (NIV).

Lodged in Chet's mind was, *God will hold me accountable.*

When Operation Rescue came to Las Vegas, Chet was convinced these "rescuers" were Christians; his pastor was among them. Three months before his retirement from the force, Chet went to the scene of the action against orders. He parked his motorcycle, gave it a pat, perhaps a gesture that *maybe we'll be parted,* and approached the group.

A friend, recently retired from the North Las Vegas Police Department, led the group. Chet took his bullhorn and pled with fellow officers not to arrest people who were doing the policemen's job— protecting innocent babies from murder. He *waxed eloquent for about two minutes,* but his supervisor was not impressed. "Chet, you're suspended. Leave this area," he ordered.

What Chet had said, he meant. He responded, "Steve, I know you don't believe they're killing babies on the other side of this door, but I do, and as a police officer, I cannot walk away from what I know to be a murder in progress."

In full uniform, Chet was the first person arrested that day. Of forty others, ten were pastors. "We had an amazing church service in the holding cell, praising God and singing. Every thirty minutes or so, a prisoner was thrown in with us. These men didn't have a chance. All heard the Word of God, and some were saved," Chet exulted.

Months later, a press conference was held on the same sidewalk where ninety-two in total, had been arrested. As the reporter asked questions, Chet was handed a six-week-old baby boy. Joshua kicked his feet and drooled all over Chet. This healthy, rambunctious baby would have been cut up in pieces before extraction from his mother's womb and then ground up in an industrial-strength garbage disposal. But Joshua was saved, and his mother was taken into Chet's church and cared for.

During an interview at God's Learning Channel, GLC, Chet explained that America's earliest abortion history began long before 1973, primarily through Margaret Sanger, the eugenicist, who founded Planned Parenthood. Much of the data he shared was taken from the documentary, "Maafa 21" which means in Swahili, "horrible death, a great slaughter" (twenty-first century). Sanger faced the American "problem" that resulted after slaves were freed. Their population had grown to 11,000,000. She promoted sterilization of those she considered "weeds, benign imbeciles, and an unwanted race" *or class of people.*

Sound familiar? The Egyptian Pharaoh instructed Hebrew midwives to kill baby boys to stop the growth of Jewish slaves. King Herod put to death all boys under age two to stop Jesus' Kingdom on earth.

Indeed, Margaret Sanger's methods became known to Adolf Hitler. He built on her model to purify the Aryan race, first by caricature and propaganda against the Jews. That would be expanded to Christians, the infirm, and the handicapped. His evil doctors practiced diabolical surgical experiments on live people, without anesthesia. Holocaust museums document the indecencies of a corrupt and depraved despot.

Zyklon gas murdered millions in death camps. How different are poisonous drugs, i.e., RU486, that kill babies in the womb? Connections between Hitler and Sanger are shocking, deadly.

Today's dehumanization of life is focused on the "unwanted, unplanned" baby. This process also accelerates toward the value of elderly citizens as "they become a burden to society." Pregnancy is not a disease or a sin. God has created every human life in His Image. Every child is an eternal being, a pre-conceived notion in the mind of God.

Chet says, "Personhood U.S.A. lays axe at the root to end abortion." Ohio, Nevada, Colorado, Oklahoma, and California have carried initiatives on their ballot to establish personhood for the least of these. Churches must engage; hold drives to get these petitions signed. Many signatures are required to meet state legislatures' requirements.

Christians must go to the government and insist personhood rights be granted to prenatal children who have no protection under the law. Then the U.S. Constitution will secure the decision just as the Supreme Court in *Roe v. Wade* has said it will do.

Chet concludes, "If we can understand where we are as a nation after forty years of legalized baby murder and turn, we can end the slaughter in a war that is biblical. If we don't, God will judge us."

"No man makes a greater mistake than he who does nothing because he could only do a little," Edmund Burke.

Contact: Chet Gallagher, Team Leader/Missionary
Personhood U.S.A.
6420 E. Tropicana Ave., Ste. 262, Las Vegas, Nevada 89122
Phone: 702-272-2279; Personhoodusa.com

CHAPTER 15

Precious Feet
Dinah Monahan

"What are those little feet?"

This simple question has saved countless babies' lives. The "little feet" are in the form of a lapel pin that depicts the exact size and shape of an unborn baby's feet at ten weeks after conception. It is a powerful visual showing the humanity of the unborn child. The creator of "The Precious Feet" is a first-generation pro-lifer named Virginia Evers.

"I saw the photo of the tiny feet of a miscarried baby held between the finger and thumb of Dr. Sacco. They moved me to tears. I thought, *if only people could see those perfect little toes, they would know that it is a baby*. The idea of the pin was an inspiration from God." said Virginia.

While Virginia felt the idea was inspired, she could not imagine the monumental impact this little pin would have worldwide.

In 1979, The "Precious Feet" were declared the International Pro-Life symbol at the Worldwide Pro-Life Symposium in Dublin, Ireland. What a great honor! But the best reward Virginia received were letters like the one from Terry of Atlanta, Georgia:

"....Our volunteer talked to both girls but felt we would lose their babies to abortion. As she was leaving, she remembered the 'Precious Feet' on her collar and gave them to one of the girls. She told her 'these are the exact size of a ten-week-old baby's feet' (the precise point of her pregnancy). Well, our volunteer came back and we all prayed, but the 'Precious Feet' had done their work—we were able to save not one but two babies! Our thanks for making the 'Precious Feet' available to us."

The greatest accolade, however, came from Carol Everett, former abortion-clinic owner, turned pro-life in Dallas, Texas:

"You know those little feet pins? Those things used to irritate me to death when I was in the abortion business. I couldn't stand them. In the grocery line, a girl of about sixteen was wearing the feet. That just drove me crazy because, of course, she was shining the truth on me. I didn't understand that then, but I hated them."

Since the idea was conceived, over fifteen million have been produced. They can be found in nearly every country in the world.

In China at the United Nations Conference on Families, National Right to Life's (NRTL) booth was overrun with people who wanted Precious Feet. NRTL also took them to the United Nation's Council on women in Istanbul, Turkey. The pins were so popular that every waiter, busboy, hotel clerk and even the master of ceremonies wore them. Everywhere the pro-abortion delegates went, they were greeted with Precious Feet on people's lapels.

This little pin also launched Virginia and husband Ellis into a business that has become the largest marketing company of pro-life products in the world. Heritage House '76 offers not only Precious Feet but everything imaginable to equip pregnancy help centers and pro-life groups and individuals.

The Evers' pro-life passion is their family legacy. Their daughter, Dinah Monahan, along with husband Mike, has dedicated her life to helping pregnant young women. For six years, her family took expectant moms into their home, often three at a time.

Says Dinah, "It makes you realize how long you've been doing this work when you take in the sixteen-year-old daughter of the first pregnant girl you took in thirty-two years before."

Tina herself was sixteen and pregnant when the Monahans took her in. They were pretty clueless and definitely did not see that this was the beginning of an exciting and challenging future God had planned. Tina chose to place her baby for adoption, went on to have two children with her husband Gary, raise his son by a previous marriage, and adopt six others. When her own daughter, Julia, reached sixteen, Tina and Gary needed some help. Tina turned to the people who had given her a home, structure, guidance, and love when *she* was sixteen and hurting."

Julia stayed with the Monahans for nine months and returned home a very different person. "Now that made me feel old," says Dinah.

The saying, "Where God leads, He provides," is Dinah's guiding principle. Her accomplishments speak to this. She is the founder of three pregnancy-help centers and a maternity home in Show Low, Arizona. The amazing thing is that one of those centers is on the White Mountain Apache Indian Reservation – the only center on a reservation in the country.

She is also the creator of "Earn While You Learn," an educational program that shifted the paradigm in pregnancy-help centers from just giving away free baby items to having clients earn them through education. Over one thousand centers employ this method.

After retiring in 2010, Dinah and Mike went on to found the first maternity home and pregnancy-help center in Ethiopia. Now the Precious Feet are saving Ethiopian babies.

While Dinah's passion spans thirty-five years of involvement with pregnant young women, Mike and their son Brandon run The Heritage House '76. When Brandon and his four siblings were little, they helped their parents pin Precious Feet onto cards. The Heritage House, a "mom-and-pop" operation, was in their grandparents' home down the street.

The Heritage House '76 is much larger and high tech, but some things don't change. You can go in there and find Brandon's children sitting around a table pinning Precious Feet just like their daddy did thirty years ago.

Being pro-life is about loving babies. For Dinah and Mike, it is a love celebration every day. Their five children, all actively pro-life, have given them twenty-one grandchildren. Three of them were adopted from Ethiopia. At ninety-three, Virginia lives in her home in Taylor and still crusades for the unborn whenever she can. Four generations are committed to saving unborn babies' lives and offering new lives to their mothers. This is the Evers' legacy of life.

Contact: Dinah Monahan
Heritage House '76
919 S. Main St., Snowflake, AZ 85937
Phone: 800-858-3040; www.hh76.com

CHAPTER 16

The Last Chance
Brian Gibson

They refused to leave until all abortions stopped. Ninety minutes later, police placed them under arrest. Criminal trespass was the charge.

On March 5, 1981, four local college students entered the Planned Parenthood abortion facility in St. Paul, MN and took strategic places inside the waiting room. The young men planned this endeavor despite efforts made educationally and legislatively to end abortion; real unborn human beings were being torturously dismembered—systematically killed—each and every day.

Innocent preborn babies, then and now, need an immediate response to save their lives. After much prayer and thought, the men acted. Yet once released from jail, they realized this type of activity was unsustainable. It could not be repeated daily if they were to try to save lives.

A burning passion and desire to intervene for lives scheduled for abortion led them to engage in what they would later name sidewalk counseling. The same zeal and energy for life used to organize the "sit-in" resulted in daily sidewalk counseling at Planned Parenthood.

More than thirty-three years later, over 2,900 saved lives have been documented. Pro-Life Action Ministries has finely tuned their sidewalk-counseling efforts, seeking to save every life possible. The purpose of sidewalk counseling is in keeping with the reason those young men courageously walked into that abortuary in 1981. Unborn babies are killed every day. Sidewalk counseling's response is a dedicated effort whose purpose has never changed.

Sidewalk counseling is not about closing abortion mills though they may impact that reality, or becoming the new John the Baptist or other prophetic voice. It is not to demonstrate, picket, or display pro-life signage. Sidewalk counseling is not about preaching. All of these have their place and should be employed as proper responses to abortion. This is Pro-Life Action Ministries' philosophy.*

Prayer vigils and rallies can be dynamic witnesses for human life and can reinforce a powerful spiritual dimension. Pro-Life Action Ministries' 2011 Good Friday vigil had attendance of more than 2,500 and in 2012, 3,200 faithful pro-lifers joined together. Though successful, enriching many, these vigils interfered with our main objective—saving lives.

All other activities must be set aside so that babies' lives can be saved in that critical hour. Conversations other than with the mothers or their companions can distract. All attention is riveted to prevent the destruction of the lives of the unborn.

In order to do that, sidewalk counselors' focus must be on the abortion-minded mothers. At times the outcome depends on the mind or heart of a boyfriend, girlfriend, or other family member. There may be offensive actions of a clinic employee or escort directed toward the counselors. It is a strategy of the pro-aborts to stir-up a confrontation while the mother slips inside. Personal emotions must be checked.

Sidewalk counselors must be spiritually-mature individuals of prayer, dedicated to growing deeper in their prayer life, and open to the Holy Spirit. Every encounter requires constant prayer to engage in this difficult mission. Babies' lives hang in the balance.

The mother deserves absolute, committed attention. Sidewalk counselors are to be approachable—from demeanor to words, dress, and literature. A sincere smile may win her trust. Anything that interferes with this focus must be ignored.

Engaging the woman in conversation and listening well elicits the best response. It is the Holy Spirit who guides, often finding vulnerability in the heart of the mother.

There is no room for deception. Words must ring true in her heart and mind to overcome what she is being told by clinic workers, escorts, family, boyfriend—all who would persuade her that abortion is her only choice. Here is the golden opportunity to exercise the voice of reason.

Sidewalk Counselors have many helps. They don't come to the sidewalks the first time, expecting to have all knowledge and irresistible clichés. What they do come with is a desire to save the life of a baby. That takes precedence over evangelizing the woman at this time. It takes precedence over conversations with fellow sidewalk counselors, escorts, workers, or passersby.

Pro-Life Action Ministries has developed wonderful literature that can be shown by the sidewalk counselor reading along with the mother or those who accompany her. Often it is only the literature, perhaps reluctantly accepted as the person brushes aside the counselor. In the clinic's waiting room, God can act through these tools. The hands and prayers of those wielding the tools have frequently led the mother to rethink her decision.

Sidewalk Counselors often are able to connect the mothers with the helps provided through crisis pregnancy centers. This teamwork bears great fruit as the mother's decision is reinforced, blessing both organizations.

"Though we give our best, yet babies still die. We mourn the babies lost. Mothers ignore our pleas, escorts/workers scoff at us, and passersby may even scream at us. We have no idea the good our great God is accomplishing through us. Babies, even rejected by their own mothers in life, have a friend standing up for them in death, as they reach the arms of Jesus."

"We are therefore, Christ's ambassadors, as though God were making his appeal through us" II Corinthians 5:20, (NIV).

Pro-Life Action Ministries, Inc., a premiere sidewalk counseling ministry, has many peers across America, either laboring on the streets in conjunction with established organizations, or independently called to areas where they join the Lord to defend the unborn babies.

Many resources, literature, and training are available. Pro-Life Action Ministries holds an annual Sidewalk Counseling Symposium each summer. They have Branch Offices in Duluth, MN and Orlando, FL. Prayers, volunteers, and donations are gratefully accepted.

Above article adapted from material formulated by Brian Gibson.

*Not all sidewalk counselors have the same philosophy regarding signage, evangelistic efforts, or preaching, but all are united in purpose.

Contact: Brian Gibson, Executive Director
Pro-Life Action Ministries, Inc.
P.O. Box 75368
Saint Paul MN 55175-0368
Phone: 651-771-1500
Website: plam.org

CHAPTER 17

A Voice That Cannot Be Stopped
M. Susan Pine

During her thirty years absent from the church, Susan Pine had two abortions. She later reflected, "I didn't know if abortion was the right thing to do, but no one told me it was wrong."

When she returned to church, no reference to abortion was ever mentioned at Mass.

One morning outside her church, Susan was confronted by a woman who asked her to pray to end abortion. The encounter was so unexpected. "I didn't know how to respond to this woman," Susan recalled.

When the lady saw Susan's hesitation, she asked, "Could you pray for the mothers then?"

Susan thought, *I could do that.* But walking away, another thought came, *Could I pray for the mothers and not the babies?* "I walked over to the Adoration Chapel and got on my knees and asked, *"God what do you think of abortion?"*

His answer came over the next several days. "Now, not only did I realize what I had done was wrong, but for the first time I was truly sorry. I grieved the loss of my children." As a result, Susan has given her life and service to end abortion. This scripture found its home in her heart:

Speak up for those who cannot speak for themselves, for the rights of all who are destitute" Proverbs 31:8, (NIV).

She met Fr. Tom Eutenuer in 1988 when he became a priest. A year or so later, Susan accompanied Fr. Tom to the local abortion center and regularly engaged in street activism.

"We prayed and offered help from the beginning. I remember it as my first admission that I had had an abortion, but only to a mother in the hope of saving her child."

Susan organized Fr. Tom's pilgrimages to Our Lady of Guadalupe. She continued to sidewalk counsel and also participated in protests at abortionists' homes or medical offices. These exposures within the community had their impact. Neighbors and patients were either dismayed or outraged.

"Initially there was more negative response than positive to these campaigns, but through the years it has gained positive support. America has become much more pro-life. We are winning."

October 2000, Susan founded FACE Life, Inc, a 501(c3) non-profit. She has been its president ever since. At that time Fr. Tom became President of Human Life International and moved to Virginia.

"Although we missed Fr. Tom, there was no question that we would continue. Shortly thereafter, through fund-raising efforts on the part of three Catholic Schools, a foundation, and private donations, FACE Life acquired a Mobile Counseling and Education Unit that serves the West Palm Beach area."

FACE Life also partnered with pro-lifers in Orlando to provide sonograms outside abortion centers. Many CPC's, crisis pregnancy centers, have their own ultrasounds, but for those pregnant girls and women who never enter a CPC, their only sonogram may be the one used by the abortionist as he dismembers their babies during abortion.

Many babies have been saved by FACE Life's ultrasound availability. Statistics show that over 90% of women who see a sonogram of their preborn baby will choose life.

Other opportunities opened up and Susan broadcast a weekly hour-long radio program reporting local and national pro-life news. In addition, she made local television appearances, held newspaper interviews, and gave college talks. She has debated Planned Parenthood on National TV (Fox News, "Dayside"), and has appeared on the *Lou Dobbs' Show*. Susan appeared on video with Life Dynamics, Denton, Texas.

A few years ago, Susan successfully sued the Presidential Women's Center and two West Palm Beach Police Officers for wrongful arrest. Due to terms of the settlement, she cannot reveal the amount adjudged in her favor. Susan followed a biblical example:

> *"When you are brought before synagogues, rulers and authorities, do not worry about how you will defend yourselves or what you will say, for the Holy Spirit will teach you at that time what you should say"* Luke 12:11-12, (NIV).

The City of West Palm Beach attempted to establish a buffer zone around Presidential Women's Center. Cases like these are abridgments of Constitutional free speech rights. Susan sued and won again.

Her most recent in a string of legal battles involved U.S. Attorney General Eric Holder over an event that occurred Nov 19, 2009. Eric Holder sued Susan under the FACE Act, Freedom of Access to Clinic Entrances. It was one of those "out-of-the-blue" stealth attacks.

The judge thought the abortion center and the Department of Justice, DOJ, conspired against Susan. The DOJ lacked evidence to incriminate her, and Susan won. Their only evidence was a police officer's testimony that did not agree with the abortion center's complaint.

The Liberty Counsel, a Christian legal organization, argued on Susan's behalf. She was awarded $120,000 for attorney fees, a stunning defeat for the Obama Administration.

FACE Life maintains a 24-hour hotline for pregnant women and their families.

FACE Life organized the two first local "Forty Days for Life" efforts and continues to sponsor them today. Intensive volunteer participation brings awareness to the community and media that people and peaceful, non-confrontational prayers saves babies. Twice a year, in spring and fall, "Forty Days for Life" changes lives—babies survive, abortion workers leave their jobs, and families are united. The most recent Forty Days for Life in West Palm Beach had over 600 volunteers.

Susan's constant focus through FACE Life has been Presidential Women's Center and Planned Parenthood. Presidential Women's Center, a private company whose owner has a celebrity status in the abortion industry, has felt the impact of Susan and her volunteers' presence.

Presidential's liberal legal teams consistently lose each time they go on the offensive.

FACE Life also staffs the sidewalks at Planned Parenthood. God shines through Susan and her team. "It is He who saves."

Contact: M. Susan Pine
FACE Life, Inc.
PO Box 15601
West Palm Beach FL 33416
Phone: 561- 641-0065
Yourfriend@FACELife.org

CHAPTER 18

States of Refuge
Pastor Rusty Thomas

"Lest the avenger of blood pursue and kill an innocent person," God created *Cities of Refuge* to provide asylum for the accused while his innocence or guilt was established.

Operation Save America, OSA, has embarked on a new national vision named: *States of Refuge, Operation: First Abortion-Free States.*

According to God's Word, innocent blood cries out to God for justice. In ancient Israel, six Levitical cities were set apart for refuge in cases of questionable death. It was also designed to protect Israel from blood guiltiness. OSA is expanding this biblical model, to protect America against blood guiltiness in our day. They believe States of Refuge is a vision whose time has come:

> *"And the LORD answered me, and said, write the vision, and make it plain on tables, that he may run that reads it. For the vision is yet for an appointed time, but at the end it shall speak, and not lie; though it tarry, wait for it; because it will surely come, it will not tarry"* Habakkuk 2:2-3, (NIV).

Habakkuk says, *"Write the vision and make it plain."* OSA is promoting this national campaign, hoping others will read, bear witness, and run with the vision until it comes to pass.

- OSA's ultimate goal is to end the American holocaust—a holocaust which has invoked God's just wrath upon our nation as innocent blood cries out to Him from the ground.

- OSA's strategy is to establish "abortion-free" states among the five states, Arkansas, Mississippi, North Dakota, South Dakota, and Wyoming which each have one abortion clinic remaining, defiling our land. These locations represent the abortion industry at its weakest and most vulnerable points. For the Church, it represents the greatest opportunity for victory.

How is this victory advanced? After research and intelligence gathering, OSA conducts national and regional events with other Christian/Pro-Life ministries of like faith. These ministries create a wave-after-wave impact to free targeted states from the sin of blood guiltiness.

- OSA's plan is to confront the altars of Moloch with every possible God-honoring, peaceful, lawful means and defeat this evil drowning of America in a sea of bloody perversion.

God's biblical mandate reads:

"For though we live in the world, we do not wage war as the world does. The weapons we fight with are not the weapons of the world. On the contrary, they have divine power to demolish strongholds. We demolish arguments and every pretension that sets itself up against the knowledge of God, and we take captive every thought to make it obedient to Christ. And we will be ready to punish every act of disobedience, once your obedience is complete" 2 Corinthians 10:3-6, (NIV).

The Pro-life infrastructure of human resources and Christian patronage is already in place. What has been lacking is a concentrated, coordinated effort to apply godly pressure at these exposed areas. *States of Refuge, Operation: First Abortion-Free States* seeks to provide an overarching mission to inspire like-minded, Christian/Pro-life ministries to come alongside and head in a parallel direction to achieve a common goal.

- OSA's mission unashamedly appropriates the cause of pre-born children in the name of Jesus Christ, employing only Biblical principles. The Cross of Christ is its strategy; the repentance of His Church, its ultimate goal.
- OSA believes Jesus Christ is the only answer to the abortion holocaust. There are no cheap political solutions to the holocaust presently ravaging our nation. Like slavery before it, abortion is preeminently a Gospel issue. The Cross of

Christ is the only solution. "Abortion will come to an end when the Church of Jesus Christ makes up her mind it will end—and not one second sooner," declares Rev. Flip Benham, National Director of OSA.

- OSA believes we have abandoned God's truth for men's vain philosophies. Thus, idolatrous practices, such as abortion and homosexuality, have proliferated under our watch. These abominations have reached heaven and now God's hand is stretched out against the land of the free and the home of the brave. The Apostle Paul states the dilemma well: *"Professing themselves to be wise, they became fools...Who changed the truth of God into a lie, and worshipped and served the creature more than the Creator, who is blessed forever. Amen"* Romans 1:22-25, (NIV).

As the Church changes her heart toward preborn children, God Himself *will hear from heaven, forgive our sin, and bring healing to our land.* According to OSA, "We become to the church, to our city, and to our nation, living parables that rightly represent God's heart toward His helpless children."

In keeping with its mission, OSA is not waiting for the President, the Congress, or the U.S. Supreme Court to save America and stop the shedding of innocent blood. Beyond politics' hit-or-miss solutions, the Church must rise up and take her rightful place at the gates of hell.

Rather than retreat in times of darkness, "Therefore, go and make disciples of all nations" Matthew 28:18-19a, (NIV).

"We are to march forward with a heavenly vision, empowered by God's Word, and the anointing of His Holy Spirit" Acts 26:12-23, (NIV).

"On this rock I will build my church, and the gates of Hades will not overcome it" Matthew 16:18, (NIV).

"Where there is no revelation, the people cast off restraint, but blessed is he who keeps the law" Proverbs 29:18, (NIV).

There is a direct connection between our moral and spiritual state and the litany of woe upon our bloodstained land. States of Refuge is part of a Kingdom strategy for taking back the gates of our land. States of Refuge attempts to give God cause to show mercy towards America once again.

Adapted from "States of Refuge, Operation: First Abortion-Free States" brochure with permission from Rev. Rusty Lee Thomas, evangelist, author, teacher, home-schooling father, Founder of Elijah Ministries; and Assistant Director of Operation Save America. Rusty gives law to hard-hearted sinners and grace to broken sinners, following Christ's example.

Contact: States of Refuge
P.O. Box 3126,
Waco TX 76707
www.statesofrefuge.org
mail@statesofrefuge.org
Phone: 704-933-3414

CHAPTER 19

Not One Penny
Art Ally

Does the way we invest our money truly reflect our convictions about the evils of abortion and a variety of other related moral issues? This chapter examines the abortion issue from a different perspective.

Consider carefully your answer to this question: "If God be over us, we must yield Him Universal obedience in all things. He must not be over us in one thing and under us in another, but must be over us in everything," wrote Peter Bulkely, one of America's earliest influential Puritan preachers.

Although God's Word is replete with His admonitions about the blessings and judgment promised His people as a result of their obedience or disobedience, there is one particular portion of scripture that ought to scare the daylights out of us. While Abraham minded his own business up in Canaan, God spoke to him in Genesis 15:13-16 and basically told him that his descendants would be enslaved 400 years after which they would come out and take possession of the promised land (Canaan). He concluded:

> *"For the inequity of the Amorites is not yet complete"* Genesis 15:16, (NKJV).

Once the Amorites reached a certain level of wickedness and evil....when child sacrifice, homosexuality, and sexual immorality of all kinds became sufficiently widespread and accepted by the Amorites, then God acted. God brought Abraham's descendants, the Israelites, into the land where the Amorites lived. The Amorites who weren't enslaved by the Hebrews were cast out.

Throughout the ages, when a nation became depraved and debauched beyond God's endurance, that nation bore His terrible judgment. Whether it was WWII Germany, or some of the Middle Eastern nations that continuously bedevil Israel, or some currently-godless European nations near financial collapse, time inevitably arrives when God takes action.

What about America?

- How much longer will God allow our modern version of child sacrifice, abortion, to go on as an acceptable national policy?
- How much longer will God allow homosexuality to be glorified to the point that some church denominations openly market to gays, and more ordain them as servants of God?
- How much longer will God allow a relatively few on this planet to live where having only one car and one color TV set is called 'poverty,' while the majority goes to bed hungry every night?
- How much longer will God allow us to strip Him from every governmental facility, school, and activity in our nation?

Therefore, when it comes to abortion, if God owns it all (and He does), and we are simply His stewards (and we are), how much of His money does He want invested in abortion? Hence, the title of this chapter: *Not One Penny!*

Unfortunately, although Scripture says more about money and stewardship than any other subject—over 2,300 verses—the majority of us get nearly 100% of our training in handling money from the world's view. This perspective seems always in direct opposition to God.

This is why The Timothy Plan wrote a Biblical Stewardship Study Series which is available for individual or group study. The course is also offered online through Southwestern Baptist Theological Seminary, complete with transferrable graduate degree credits (www.biblicalstewardship.org). Although this course exposes the link between investing and abortion, here is an explanation for those who do not take the course.

When you invest in stocks or bonds (or mutual funds which are simply packaged stock or bond investments), you actually become part owner of/or creditor to the companies in which you invest. You would probably be shocked to learn just how many of these companies are overtly or covertly supporting or funding abortion, pornography, or other anti-family, anti-life agendas.

Without naming names, here is an example of one of the largest, most widely-held mutual funds in the investment industry with $39 billion in assets. The following table reflects the percentage of this fund's total assets that are invested in companies that fund, support or are involved in:

- Abortion - 44.7%
- Pornography - 15.2%
- Anti-Family Entertainment - 22.9%
- Non-traditional married lifestyles - 78.6%
- Alcohol - 2.1%
- Casino Gambling - .7%

The question is how could a pro-life, pro-family investor own shares of such a fund? Its answer? They probably don't know. But the good news is there are now tools and investments available to help them know and enable better investment decisions.

Being an obedient follower of Christ is not an easy road. While trying to be *Biblically Responsible,* investment decisions might even seem overwhelming.

With the advent of state-of-the-art research and screening tools, investors now have access to more information regarding the moral makeup of publically-traded companies than previously was available. One premier service currently accessible to investors and financial planners is offered by eVALUEator Services, LC. The service provides reports that shows how much money *every* mutual fund has invested in companies involved in abortion, pornography, and other offensive activities that contradict traditional Judeo-Christian values.

Without compromise, competitive rates of return, that don't support or profit from ownership in companies involved in these activities, are available.

The pioneer company that spearheaded Biblically Responsible Investing is the Timothy Plan founded by its President, Art Ally. Started in 1994, the Timothy Plan, designed and developed a family of mutual funds that will not invest in any company directly or indirectly involved in areas of abortion, pornography, anti-family entertainment, or promoting non-traditional married lifestyles. Also included are alcohol, tobacco, and casino gambling.

Check the following websites for more information on this issue:

www.screenitcleanit.com

www.biblicalstewardship.org

www.timothyplan.com

Or call 1-800-846-7526 for a free prospectus for any Timothy Plan® fund, which contains more complete information about the management company, management fees, charges, and expenses. Please read it carefully before investing, to consider the investment objectives, risks, charges, and expenses. The Timothy Plan is distributed by Timothy Partners, Ltd. Member FINRA.

Contact: Art Ally, President
The Timothy Plan
1055 Maitland Center Commons, #100
Maitland FL 32751
Phone: 407-644-1986

CHAPTER 20

180
Pastor Ray Comfort

Why do you think Adolf Hitler killed so many Jews? Some think that it was because he had his paintings rejected by a mainly Jewish panel at an art school in Vienna. A couple of other theories are that he may have been bitter because a Jewish prostitute gave him a sexually-transmitted disease, or he was jealous because some Jews were able to make money while Germany was economically depressed.

But that doesn't make sense. Perhaps a man could become angry for any of those reasons and take his anger out on some Jewish person by murdering him. Or it could still make sense if he took a gun and murdered a family of six Jews, or a handful of Jewish co-workers. But to kill 600 would be crazy, or 6,000 would be insanely out of proportion. Adolf Hitler killed six *million* Jews, his "final solution to the problem!"There has to be something more behind this—and there is an explanation that makes sense.

On April 26, 1938, all Jews, except for the very poor, were forced by law to disclose their wealth. If Jews refused to reveal their wealth in detail, their property could be confiscated and they could get up to ten-years hard labor in prison! No doubt there was compliance from millions of Jews across Germany. *They were actually signing their own death warrant and that of their families.*

Every time Hitler killed a Jewish family, he seized their assets. A "Decree for the Reporting of Jewish Owned Property" was dated April 26, 1938. Deputy for the Four-Year Plan, General Field Marshal Goering, enforced the plan aided by The Reich Minister of the Interior,

Wilhelm Frick. To Hitler went the spoils; he got their house, their car, their savings, their jewelry, their insurance policies, their paintings, their bonds, the gold out of their teeth, the clothes off their backs, and the hair from their heads.

Hitler raked in *billions* of dollars from killing Jewish families. And when you kill an entire family, no one is left to complain. Experts now tell us that thirty percent of Hitler's massive war machine was financed directly by Jewish blood money.

In the 1930's Germany was deeply in debt, runaway inflation, and a forty-per-cent unemployment rate. They needed a savior, and Hitler stepped up to the plate.

Just as the marginalization of the Jews was financially prosperous for der Fuehrer, "women's choice" has become a cash cow for the abortion industry.

Another mystery is why the abortion industry in America is so zealous for "women's rights" when it comes to "choice." Is it because they have the same incendiary incentive?

They have a similar solution to "the problem."

You don't need to look for smoke billowing from a chimney to find a concentration clinic in your area. Just Google in the words: *abortion, prices*, and your zip code, You will find one not far from where you live. If you want your sixteen-week baby killed in the womb, according to current prices, it will cost $690. Your nineteen-week-old baby's killing just three weeks later, will jump to a massive $2,690.

The abortionist's wages are for fifteen to twenty-minutes work. He just has to rip off the baby's head, arms, and legs, and pull them out—along with the remaining bloody torso. He needs only to assemble everything on a table afterwards to make sure the entire body is out of the womb and drop the parts into the trash. When he does that ten to fifteen times, he takes home $10,000--$15,000 for a day's work.

It has nothing to do with a woman's choice. That's propaganda. It's all about lining pockets, using a well-oiled government-sanctioned killing machine.

The above adapted from, *Hitler, God, and the Bible, World Net Daily (WND)*

Through Ray Comfort the author and the accompanying movie *"180,"* pro-life activists across the nation are being energized with a simple, truthful approach to the issue. As part of his book project he interviewed university students on video, learning that many of them were unaware of Hitler's evil extremism.

Comfort, when asking them specific questions, was able to convince them to take another view of abortion in America. He asked if the students, at the point of a Nazi gun, would use a bulldozer to shovel Jews into a burial pit even if they were alive. Most said they would refuse.

He then asked a correlating question about abortion: "Do you think it's a baby in the womb?" "Just when is it all right to kill that baby?"

The result was a sensational 30-minute documentary, "*180*," which has been viewed online some 2.4 million times and has sold hundreds of thousands more. The title, *180*, refers to the 180-degree turn most take after being exposed to the truth.

"Babies are now being born that have been saved by the movie. A woman on Santa Monica pier back in October was secretly pregnant, very distressed and considering an abortion," Comfort said. "She was given a DVD, watched *180* in her car, burst into tears, and decided to keep her child." After baby Amanda Mae was born, the mother contacted Comfort.

Ray Comfort, a best-selling author of more than sixty books, Founder/President/CEO of Living Waters Publications, relocated from New Zealand to Southern California in the late 1980s, introducing pastors and churches to a biblical teaching, *Hell's Best Kept Secret.* Overwhelming response took Ray's Living Waters Publications (LWP) ministry to another level. LWP is recognized internationally, reaching the lost and equipping Christians with every necessary resource to fulfill the Great Commission. With actor Kirk Cameron, he co-hosts the television program, "The Way of the Master" which airs in seventy countries.

WND EXCLUSIVE: *This Baby Alive Because of a Video? April 23, 2012*

Contact: Evangelist Ray Comfort
Living Waters
9819 Arkansas Street
Bellflower CA 90706
www.livingwaters.com; www.180movie.com
Phone: 562-207-9300; 800-437-1893

CHAPTER 21

The Least of These
Cal Zastrow

"We didn't just talk or pray about babies being murdered by butchers, we went and stopped them. We *rescued*. We didn't just write position papers against child-sacrifice, we went and peacefully sat in front of the doors of the killing centers and prevented them from slaughtering children," Cal Zastrow refines his testimony into a priceless nugget.

Cal never felt more like a follower of Christ in his life than when actually acting like Jesus. He laid his own personal safety aside and prevented the murder of babies who were scheduled to die. Other *rescuers* have expressed similar experiences.

In April 1992, there were six surgical abortuaries in Buffalo, NY killing thousands of pre-born babies yearly. Later-term babies were murdered weekly in Children's Hospital. But now the number of surgical abortuaries in Buffalo has been reduced to one, and Children's Hospital stopped killing babies many years ago.

Upset by their lack of *business*, the baby-murderers had the police arrest and throw the peaceful anti-abortionists in jail. Women also risked arrest. Their number was unknown, but 197 men were hauled off together. A few of the police beat, stepped on, dragged, or choked some of their captives. Most spent the next twenty-four days incarcerated together.

Before being farmed out to multiple jails and prisons, all the men spent the first nine days in the asbestos-filled dungeon of the Niagara Street Armory.

Cal would later reminisce, "I've been to lots of Christian retreats, meetings, and Bible college chapels. Today marks the twentieth anniversary of the best *retreat* I've ever attended."

It wasn't the fancy cuisine, professional program, or ample accommodations that made their *retreat* memorable. It was the power of the Holy Spirit that strengthened them through their trials. When the sadistic policeman, Captain Vaughan, locked them out of the bathrooms for hours, they worshipped Jesus. When the guards taunted and threatened, they worshipped Jesus.

Despite filth, deprivations, and lack of sleep, those incarcerated for their Christian principles praised their glorious King, singing "All Hail the Power of Jesus' Name." In the face of demonic tyrants, those men felt the awesome power of their Creator and could not stop praising their Lord and Master.

A cell mate of Cal's was old Frank Sync. His cot was side-by-side with Cal's for the first eight days. Frank had rescued Jews from death camps after he and his Army platoon landed in Normandy and defeated the Nazis. Cal felt honored to be in his presence.

Young and old, rescue brothers, jail brothers, they bore their imprisonment with selfless acts of mercy. They shared the few Bibles that had been smuggled in. They shared food rations, limited water, and their lives. Some men lost jobs, had family members turn against them, and churches disown them for carrying the Cross. In their suffering, they encouraged one another. They found Jesus was all they needed.

None will forget the foot-washing service, Pastor Johnny Hunter's sermon, Chet Gallagher's testimony, or the Styrofoam-cup-cross. The move of God's Spirit during the Buffalo *revival* changed Cal. He was not alone. Cal returned to his house of worship with a fire burning deep in his heart to stop the slaughter of babies. He would never be content to seek the safety of the pew.

Like half of those in the New Testament's Hall of Faith in Hebrews chapter 11, the apostles, John the Baptist, and the Lord Himself, Cal has been arrested and jailed for prayerful and peaceful Christian action. His incarceration for loving his neighbor is in the tradition of men like John Bunyan, Dietrich Bonhoeffer, Alan Keyes, and Martin Luther King Jr. His longest jail sentence, of ninety days in the

Saginaw County Jail, Michigan, leads Cal to conclude that going to jail isn't as bad as being dismembered by Planned Parenthood.

Being pro-life is socially and religiously acceptable, but actually stopping baby-murder through peaceful interposition, is often misunderstood. Those who think that this American holocaust will end from their comfortable offices and church buildings are woefully mistaken.

"The question is not, 'What will this cost me?' The question is: 'What will it cost me to disobey Christ's command to love my neighbor as myself?'" This is Cal's personal creed.

Loving your neighbor includes the tiny person in the womb, the one who has been denied personhood by both the law and the culture. Even famed children's book author, Dr. Seuss, got it right when he wrote, "A person is still a person no matter how small."

Cal and his wife Trish began their pro-life activities in the late 1980s at a Christian pregnancy-resource center in Flint, Michigan. They began rescuing babies through peaceful sit-ins at abortion mills in 1991.

Cal can't know how many babies have been saved through his family's missionary efforts, but co-workers know that the Zastrows have personally saved hundreds of children scheduled to be killed by Planned Parenthood and other abortionists.

"Whatever the number," Cal says, "it isn't enough. We will not stop fighting until abortion in America is abolished, just as slavery was."

Besides being a full-time Christian missionary with his family on the streets in front of aborturaries, Cal Zastrow is one of the pioneers of the Personhood Movement. He was a leading force in Colorado's historic statewide personhood campaign which has ignited personhood efforts nationwide.

He spearheads efforts to amend State Constitutions to define the word "person" to include all pre-born children and protect their God-given right to life. Not content with legislation, churches, or pro-life strategies that permit the murdering of some babies, he works to get others to recognize the humanity of all these children, and protect them by love and by law.

There is no cost too great to end this age-based discrimination and restore the legal protections of personhood to the pre-born.

Contact: Cal Zastrow
Phone: 601-454-4819
calzastrow@hotmail.com

CHAPTER 22

Without Apology
Mark Crutcher

Some pro-lifers tread lightly, are so politically correct as to avoid offending others. They never run afoul of fence-sitters. A few years ago, there was a growing trend among those who relied on financial assistance from churches to sanitize their arguments. They tried to cushion folks from real-life depictions of aborted babies to avoid making post-abortive women uncomfortable. They never mentioned abortion during church services.

Their fund raisers, programs, and public advocacy leaned toward "Celebrate Life." They threw happy, celebratory baby showers that received generous bounty for their clients, but omitted mention of the other babies who would never wear those onesies and never be strolled through the mall.

They considered removing words like abortion, victims, murder, and anti-abortion from the pro-life lexicon. Such a move would nearly equivocate the-culture-of-death's sanitized words—*product of conception, termination of a pregnancy, and women's choice.*

Controversial, hard line, or adversarial, one organization has been edgy from the beginning. Life Dynamics lives up to its name, leaving nuance and finesse behind. They are Pro-life: Without compromise. Without exception. Without apology.

Mark Crutcher, the man behind the vision, trod where no one else had gone before—most often under the radar.

Committed to the pro-life movement, Mark went full time in 1986 after years as an outspoken, uncompromised opponent of legalized abortion. At that time, he created the Life Activist Seminar and eventually trained more than 15,000 pro-life activists across the U.S. and Canada. In 1992, he founded Life Dynamics, acknowledged as one of the most innovative and professional pro-life organizations in America.

Life Dynamics created an extensive litigation/support system that helps women sue abortionists who injure or sexually assault them. Mark's group also carries out aggressive direct mail campaigns within the medical community, designed to discourage doctors and nurses from entering the abortion business. Life Dynamics developed strategies and products for crisis pregnancy centers which are used extensively.

Mark may be best known for his bold undercover operations that have exposed shocking and illegal activities inside the abortion industry. A few years ago, a Life Dynamics sting caught Planned Parenthood and others in the abortion industry operating a nationwide pedophile-protection ring.

Here's a segment from Mark's in-depth report: *According to the most reliable studies among girls fifteen and younger who become pregnant, between sixty and eighty percent of them are impregnated by adult men. In America today, we have reached the point where a junior high school girl is more likely to become pregnant by an adult than by someone close to her own age.*

Another sting documented how abortion clinics make extra profit selling babies' body parts: *In response to information released by Life Dynamics, on March 8, 2000, the ABC News program 20/20 aired a segment about the marketing of baby parts from children killed during abortions. On the following day there was a Congressional hearing on the same issue.*

The success of Mark's covert surveillance efforts led one New York newspaper to label Life Dynamics "The CIA of the Pro-Life Movement."

In 1996, Mark authored the book, *Lime 5*, an exposé that has become the recognized standard for people who want a deeper look inside the American abortion industry. Among his numerous other writings is the pro-life handbook, *On Message*, as well as *Access, the Key to Pro-Life Victory* and the pocket guide, *Pro-Life Answers,* and many hard-hitting flyers put to good use by pro-lifers everywhere.

Articles about Mark and Life Dynamics have been published in both *Time* and *Newsweek*. He has written for *The Christian American, All About Issues*, and Focus on the Family's *Citizen* magazine. *ABC World News Tonight, NBC Nightly News, the CBS Evening News, Fox News, Nightline, 20/20, the O'Reilly Factor, and the 700 Club* have featured him as well as many local and national television news outlets. He contributes regularly to *World Net Daily, American Family Radio, Family News in Focus,* and the *USA Radio Network.*

In 1999, Mark launched *Life Talk*, the nation's first pro-life television talk show. Today, his co-hosts include Father Frank Pavone, National Director of Priests for Life; Cherie Johnson, Troy Newman, National leader of Operation Rescue, Dr. Johnny Hunter, president of America's largest black pro-life organization, and Janet Morana, co-founder of Silent No More.

Awards presented to Mark Crutcher are:

2002, the first annual *Cardinal Von Galen Award* from Human Life International.

2004, the *Cardinal O'Connor Pro-Life Hall of Fame Award.*

2009, the *Blogger of the Year Award from* American Life League.

Among Life Dynamics' latest projects was a revolutionary campaign designed to increase African-American participation in the pro-life movement. One part of this effort is a stunning documentary film called *Maafa 21,* which, in just over two hours, leaves no doubt that the driving force behind the legalization of abortion was eugenics and racial genocide. More than 20,000 copies of *Maafa 21* have been distributed on DVD and is being shown at theaters, churches, college campuses, and conventions nationally.

On two occasions it has been shown at the Congressional Visitors Center in Washington, DC. In March 2010, *Maafa 21* was the featured film at the Jubilee Festival in Selma, Alabama, commemorating the forty-fifth anniversary of the march over the Edmund Pettus Bridge. Many consider this historic event, known as "Bloody Sunday" to have been a turning point for the American Civil Rights Movement.

Life Dynamics is your go-to place for an in-depth education of all things pertaining to pro-life. Check out Mark's blogs. Its extensive array of scholarly essays will enlighten and inspire you.

Contact: Mark Crutcher
Life Dynamics Inc.
204 Cardinal Dr
Denton TX 76209
Phone: 940-380-8800; Fax: 940-380-8700
www.lifedynamics.com
Toll-free order line for LDI donations or products1-800-800-
LIFE.

CHAPTER 23

Victim or Sinner?
Michele Herzog

"On January 22, 1973, abortion was legalized. We cheered the victory."

Michele Herzog and her friends didn't look at this as an abortion issue cleverly disguised as women's rights. They bought the lie.

"I thought, *this is a wonderful stride for women, but I would never do it*. I was above that."

At twenty, Michele headed down a rocky path. She experimented with drugs, alcohol, and an immoral lifestyle she had once abhorred. Michele was pregnant.

"The baby's father, like myself, was adrift. He didn't want the baby, but I did. My friends said, 'Are you crazy?' Reluctantly, I called the clinic—the very thing I was sure I would never do."

Michele stood in a phone booth in 1975 and cried. She fed the phone some coins. The woman sounded understanding, praised the doctor, and Michele made the appointment. With dread, she went with a girlfriend from work who also was pregnant—five-months, visibly pregnant—preparing for her child's birth.

They arrived at a two-story house. Michele walked up the stairs and went inside. She sat beside her friend and thought, *why does she get to keep her baby and I don't?*

"Michele?"

"I shuffled to the back. The abortion was a blur. Afterwards, I walked out, looked at the sky, and said, *I will never do that again.* Something had changed. I felt cold—a piece of me died along with the baby."

Later, the baby's father came to Michele's workplace and left notes on her car: "Murderer." "You killed my baby." He became so violent, Michele moved back to Florida for protection.

Did she learn her lesson? "Instead, I grew worse. Drinking, using drugs, involved in promiscuous relationships—I was in the same situation four more times. Bad decisions, wrong choices, painful outcomes. I paid someone to kill my children."

Michele looks for no sympathy. She maintains she is not a victim. She lives with the pain of her choices. "My precious innocent babies were the victims, not me."

Four a.m., June 29, 1986, God delivered Michele from drugs and drinking. Jesus Christ became her Savior and Messiah. He lifted her from the pit of hell and gave her new life. She can never praise Him enough.

But Michele's hidden sin and its guilt remained locked inside. When her pastor, Dr. D. James Kennedy, preached on the subject of abortion, Michele quietly left her pew and walked out. Afraid her new friends would reject her, she maintained silence for almost two years.

Each evening, Michele cried over her abortions. She could not understand how God could forgive her.

One night her Bible fell to the floor. It lay open at Jeremiah 29:11-13:

> *"For I know the thoughts that I think toward you, saith the LORD, thoughts of peace, and not of evil, to give you an expected end. Then shall ye call upon me, and ye shall go and pray unto me, and I will hearken unto you. And ye shall seek me, and find me, when ye shall search for me with all your heart,"* (KJV).

Michele read this and felt a twinkle of peace in the distance.

She joined a ministry to Haitian children, moved to a rough section of Miami, and lived among those she served. Some parents though drug dealers, accepted the missionaries because they loved their children.

Two missionaries returned from a pro-life rally in Tallahassee and shared their excitement. "My heart pounded as I listened to them. Internally, I held onto my abortions with clenched fists, but as His Holy Spirit convicted and nudged me, I gained every bit of strength I had and spit it out, 'I had abortions.'"

Michele expected to be thrown out of ministry, but her unconditional friends, Jodi, Rob, and Brian laid hands on her and prayed. Michele confessed her sin of abortion, "I paid someone to kill my five children!"

The Bible says in Romans 2:4: *"It's His kindness that leads us to repentance,"* (NIV).

"Truly, His kindness led me to repentance. I felt *chains* fall from me; I was now free."

Michele received post-abortion counseling at a pregnancy center in Miami. Later, Rev. Pat Mahoney of Rescue South Florida invited Michele to speak at a pro-life rally held at Coral Ridge Presbyterian Church. Many women, crying about their abortions, approached her afterwards. In that moment, Michele knew this was the path God wanted her to follow.

Michele has rescued. "Every time it seemed like the right thing to do." She served three months in the Pinellas County jail.

One inmate, a young black girl, ran up to her and said, "I went to an abortion clinic eight months ago for an abortion, saw a crowd of people, and pictures of aborted babies. I couldn't kill my baby. I have my baby boy, and I rededicated my life to Christ. I turned myself in for past crimes. Thank you for stopping me."

Another inmate who seemed familiar entered Michele's dorm. She was the abortion-clinic nurse who tried to push through the pro-lifers the day of the rescue, but was stopped by the police. Her job was to put the babies back together after each abortion. This had resulted in her continual nightmares of aborted babies. Jailed for her third drunk-driving charge, she accepted Jesus after eighteen days of Michele and her friends loving on her and sharing the Gospel.

"God our Sovereign put her in our dorm. She never went back to do abortions."

For over twenty years, Michele still speaks for unborn children. She lived ten years in Wichita where she and her family ministered outside the gates of the infamous George Tiller's late-term abortuary.

"Each time I saw ashes of the children spew out of that smoke stack as the incinerator inside his mill blasted away, my heart broke. Pieces of cremated children fell on our shoes. My resolve, my passion to restore personhood for these babies, grew stronger."

In 2010, Michele brought her pro-life activism to Central Florida, and her indefatigable energy to close all abortuaries. God will bring it to pass.

Contact: Michele Herzog
e-mail: micheleforlife@gmail.com

CHAPTER 24

The Real War Against Women
Janet Morana and Georgette Forney

Is there really such a war being waged against women in the United States? Absolutely! This war is evident nearly everywhere we look.

Turn on the television and see it raging on MTV, VH1, and CMT where rappers, rockers, and even country crooners spew misogynistic lyrics while provocatively-dressed women degrade themselves with their dancing. The war flourishes in Hollywood where the most common, sought-after role for an actress is a hooker with a heart of gold. At least one movie out of three includes a completely gratuitous sexual scene in a strip club. The entertainment media delights in women taking their clothes off for the camera. Why is there such a hunger to see accomplished, talented, beautiful women naked? Because it devalues them?

The war on women is executed in the tastefully-appointed offices of plastic surgeons reaping the rewards of a culture that values large breasts and unlined faces. Few know that most implants leak or break over time, often with devastating consequences. Should it matter?

Does it matter that hormonal contraceptives—the Pill and its descendants—are indisputably linked to increased risks of cardiovascular disease, cervical, liver, and breast cancer; blood clots, elevated blood pressure, decreased desire, sexual dysfunction, and stroke?

The Pill began its war on women in Puerto Rico in the late 1950s when tested on unsuspecting women. Some died.

"Why would anyone want to put a *Class One* carcinogen in her

88

body three out of four weeks, when she's only fertile 100 hours a month," asks Angela Lanfranchi, a New Jersey oncologist. "The Pill is bad."

Battles carry over to the media, where female politicians—liberal and conservative—are subjected to endless critiques of their clothing choices and hairstyles. No man in the political arena has ever faced these pressures, except perhaps John Edwards and his $400 haircut.

Particularly vicious is the war on women in strip clubs and on porn sets. Women violated in sometimes unspeakable ways have been trafficked from distant parts of the world. Desperation trumps common sense and women accept a stranger's offer of a good job, only to find themselves enslaved, abused, and addicted. Brothels and nude bars are full of women whose right to choose—if they ever had one—was surrendered at the border crossing. Men, whose sense of entitlement has enabled them to overlook the humanity of the women they victimize, continue feeding their greed.

While battles rage on many fronts, abortion is the nuclear weapon in the arsenal of "the war against women." Nowhere is the war waged, as effectively and horrifically, as it is in the abortion clinic where no doctor/patient relationship exists—where every abortion stops one heart and breaks another.

The women's movement of the sixties and seventies set out to prove that women can do anything men can. In many ways, that's true. But somewhere along the way women devalued their unique gift, the ability to conceive and give birth to new life. They threw it away in exchange for sexual liberation and a *get-out-of-jail-free card* if an "unplanned pregnancy" should intrude.

What a terrible trade-off for millions of women and their babies.

"I wish that in the seventies, when I was pro-choice and believed the jargon, 'My body, My Choice,' someone had told me that 'my choice' would haunt me for the rest of my life," said Leslie Brunolli of San Diego, a regional coordinator in the Silent No More Awareness Campaign.

"That choice left a devastating imprint on my life that no other choice I have ever made compares to." Thousands of women join Leslie every year to say they regret that choice. Millions more still suffer in silence.

The diabolical tragedy of this war on women is that we wage it, very often, on ourselves. For example, Chinese women in an earlier age insisted on binding their daughters' feet even though they themselves were crippled. Women in some African cultures still hold their daughters down to allow the same barbaric genital mutilation they endured. Finally and tragically, American mothers insist abortion be kept legal and accessible for their daughters.

We would love to stand with our sisters at rallies to fight this war against women, but the truth is, we are on opposite sides of the battle line.

The political fever on the subject of "a war against women," originated at the White House. It fomented outrage over a woman's supposed loss of "choice" if the Republican Presidential Candidate should win the November election. The issue, rather, is that the H.H.S. Mandate for tax-payer-funded insurance covering contraceptives, drug-inducing abortions, and surgical abortions are unacceptable to people of conscience.

In 2012, a grass-roots effort known as UniteWomen.org began building troops for nationwide rallies, but for them, the enemy is the GOP, Christians, Catholics, pro-lifers, and paternalistic white men who "want to keep women barefoot and pregnant." They see an abortion clinic and they think choice. We look at the same clinic, and we see the ultimate exploitation of women.

Until we can all recognize the true nature of this war, we will remain a nation divided. Here are some of the organizations that are part of the UnitedWomen.org coalition's "War Against Women" activities: Americans United For Separation of Church and State, Catholics for Choice, Feminist Peace, National Equal Rights Amendment Alliance, National Latina Institute for Reproductive Health, National Organization for Women, Religious Coalition for Reproductive Choice, Rock the Slut Vote, The Silver Ribbon Campaign to Trust Women, and This Slut Votes.

Janet Morana, Executive Director of Priests for Life, and Georgette Forney, President of Anglicans for Life, are the co-founders of the Silent No More Awareness Campaign. Their goals for people who have been hurt by abortion are:

- Reach out
- Educate
- Share

Adapted from the "LifeSite News" article, April 25, 2012, *Ready to Fight the Real War Against Women?*

Contacts:

Janet Morana
Phone: 888-735-3448

Georgette Forney
Phone: 800-707-6635
www.silentnomoreawareness.org

CHAPTER 25

Billboards Save Lives
Edward J. Daccarett

God got Ed's attention by closing doors.

Edward Daccarett remembers well Friday, July 13, 2009 because during the Divine Mercy Hour at 3:00- 4:00 p.m., he made a prophetic decision to shut down a profitable and interesting business he and his wife Laurie operated.

The following months, Ed's mind raced toward various opportunities, while Laurie filled in as a secretary with Temp Services.

Given the time to step back and think, Ed, active in the pro-life arena for twenty years, wondered why, despite prayers, sidewalk counseling, and genuine efforts by pro-lifers worldwide, *the man in the street* remained ignorant on the life issue. He thought of nothing else for three months.

Awake at 2:00 a.m. one morning, Ed lay in bed pondering the apathy of the masses against God's precious infants and got his answer. For the most part, pro-lifers preach only to the choir at churches, private schools, and other insular venues.

Ed knew what needed to be done: take the message to the people, especially to those outside the church. He felt the urgent message would save lives. Florida Pro-Life Billboards was birthed.

Life-CAN launched with nine major billboards on the Florida Turnpike and Interstate-95 from the Palm Beaches through the Treasure Coast. The campaign was funded out of Ed's pocket as Life-CAN was not yet incorporated as a 501 (c-3) non-profit. Waiting for funds to cover the campaign would have delayed life-saving messages at least three months. Ads were simple— "Life Begins At Conception," a toll-free hotline, and a sketch of a pre-born baby. The billboard company insisted the sketch of this pre-born baby could not have eyes, ears, nor mouth because the baby would look too human. Unimaginable!

Once Life-CAN incorporated and achieved their 501 (c-3) status, contributions flowed in supporting the billboards. Most contributors noted that they were "one-time gifts." This was unnerving, as billboard contracts require twelve-month commitments.

After many sleepless nights, Ed decided he would quantify his fears without sufficient support to see the program through. Rest came with the total expense quantified over a twelve-month period. Having left the matter in God's hands, Ed trusted Him to find the money.

Gradually the program expanded to Miami on Metro-Dade buses, Metro-rail cars, and station platforms, and billboards in the Miami/Ft. Lauderdale areas. Obviously, the Miami campaign was always bi-lingual. It had both separate English and Spanish-speaking hotlines.

Life Saver Ads expanded throughout Florida from north to south, east to west, and coast to coast. Presently, there are 150 major billboards, thirty-five exterior bus ads, and seventy-five interior bus ads. Life Saver Ads impact daily over 3.75 million persons with a positive pro-life message—more than the combined circulation of all Florida newspapers.

Life Saver Ads have assisted other states in starting similar programs or have shared artwork with pro-life organizations in Georgia, Alabama, Tennessee, South Carolina, Connecticut, Pennsylvania, and Indiana. Others are pending.

Not satisfied simply in "Life begins at Conception—Choose Life," Ed wanted a message that resonated. That was accomplished when the unborn child's humanity ultimately *became mindset*. Months later, Ed stumbled on the scientific fact that the heartbeat begins at eighteen to twenty-two days. Bingo! Ed seized upon that reality and launched a new campaign: "18 days after Conception, My Heart Started Beating!"

Ed shares, "Reports have come in from pregnancy-resource centers where pregnant mothers have said, 'tell me that I am pregnant, but not past eighteen days.' 'Why eighteen days,' ask the counselors?' The pregnant mothers say, 'Because the billboard says that the baby's heart is beating at eighteen days.'"

Each year as slight modifications keep the message fresh, the words change little. It's the single most effective pro-life message now being used by many pro-life groups within the USA and overseas also.

According to the Guttmacher Institute, the research arm for Planned Parenthood, over seventy per-cent of abortions are committed by Christians. An ad was created to reach those who profess Christianity showing Michelangelo's Sistine Chapel-rendering of God at creation pointing to a pregnant mother stating,

"Before I Created You In The Womb, I Knew You" Jeremiah 1:5, (NIV).

Another creative design to reach abortion-minded women features a multi-cultural young woman with its simple message, *"Got Pregnant? Get Help!"* that mimics abortion-clinic ads. The Bible admonishes us to be *"cunning as the serpent, but innocent as doves."*

Challenges are many and varied:

- Timid billboard company executives who refuse to put up a pro-life message for fear of complaints.
- Weather hazards such as hurricanes.
- Vandals.
- Irate feminists, pro-aborts, and post-abortive women and men.

"Our graphic designers constantly tweak designs and messages to ensure they are read by motorists traveling at 75 mph with only a three-to-five-second read. Still we press on with the truth, earnestly praying for their repentance and conversion."

"We never doubt that God uses these Life Saver ads for His greater good as we rely totally on Him:

'God's word shall not return void, but shall achieve the end for which it is sent' Isaiah 55:11, (NIV)."

Life-CAN's mission effectiveness is constantly affirmed by the toll-free hotline and visits made to pregnancy resource centers through their referrals.

Their marching orders are:

"Whatever you do for the least of the brothers and sisters, that you do for Me" Matthew 25:40, (NIV).

"Truly I say to you, to the extent that you did not do it to one of the least of these, you did not do it to me" Matthew 25:45, (NIV).

Ed Daccarett has absolutely no regrets that God opened his eyes and closed his business. He is busier than ever leading three different ministries: Life Saver Ads, Florida Pro-life Billboards; *Christian Action News*, a monthly newsletter; and Prince of Peace Catholic Radio.

Contact: Edward J. Daccarett
LifeCAN Inc.
Website, lifecan.org
5445 SW Woodham Street
Palm City FL 34990
Phone/Fax: 772-219-1144
E-mail: lifecan@juno.com

CHAPTER 26

Better than Bumper Stickers
Russ Amerling

What has happened to pro-life bumper stickers? They've been replaced by thousands of *Choose Life* license plates in twenty-nine states.

Does the average driver realize how this simple, colorful plate has made the adoption option more accessible? The benefits are four-fold:

- They raise other drivers' awareness about adoption as a better choice than abortion.
- They raise millions of dollars to assist adoptions.
- They actually reduce the cost of adoptions.
- Most importantly, they save lives.

In 1996, Florida Specialty Plates flooded the highways, raising funds for manatees, Florida panthers, and sea turtles—all endangered species—yet the most endangered species, the human baby, was absent. Is support for a football team, college alma mater, or spaying a pet a critical message? Choosing life for the pre-born is. That has been the mission of the *Choose Life* license plates from the beginning.

It all started with the vision God gave Marion County Commissioner Randy Harris in Ocala, Florida. Early in 1997 the Commission unanimously approved Randy's resolution to petition the State of Florida to create a *Choose Life* specialty license plate. His friends, Russ and Jill Amerling, helped fill the County Commission meeting hall with supporters on that day.

It was August 2000 before the license plates hit the road after Governor Jeb Bush signed the bill into law. So began this effective husband-and-wife team who have traveled over 250,000 miles across the United States assisting concerned citizens to introduce a *Choose Life* license plate to their own state legislatures. Sometimes one person has taken it to the State House.

This issue has been hotly debated in other places, and opposed by pro-abortion groups, including Planned Parenthood, American Civil Liberties Union, National Organization for Women, and Center for Reproductive Law and Policy. At this writing, the *Choose Life* license plate has been approved in twenty-nine states and the District of Columbia. Teams have been trained in sixteen more.

Passage is being held up by lawsuits in North Carolina and New York, the latter deeming it "blatantly offensive."

Despite huge sums of money being spent by opposition groups to stop *Choose Life* in the courts, currently *Choose Life* license plates have ultimately won or are winning in eleven of the twelve suits. God has multiplied time, efforts, and donations of its committed volunteers and brought stunning victories.

Could Randy or Russ and Jill have anticipated that over $20,000,000 dollars would be raised in the last thirteen years? Florida raised more than $9,420,000; Alabama, over $2,742,000, and Mississippi, over $2,541,000. Texas, Iowa, and North Dakota just released their first *Choose Life* plates, and Utah's tags are on pre-sale. Many others are pending.

The Amerlings receive testimonials from the ministries who administer proceeds from the sale of the *Choose Life* plates. Below are those who have placed for adoption, assisted financially, or adopted, making their dreams come true:

- "I recently released my daughter through an adoption plan. This has been a really good and positive experience for me. I was able to use Choose Life funds from the sale of the license plates for clothing, living expenses, and transportation expenses."
- "On her way to the abortion clinic she followed a car with a *Choose Life* license plate. As she got closer, she could not bring herself to keep her appointment. The message on the plate spoke so loudly to her. She followed through with her pregnancy and now has a nine-month-old son."

- "Teresa (not her real name) arrived at a pregnancy center in Tampa, FL and told her story to a counselor. She was coming to have an abortion and saw several *Choose Life* license plates on the ten-mile drive. When she arrived at the abortion clinic, she told Judy, the counselor, "You are a sign and seal that what I was about to do was wrong." She drove off knowing her future was going to be rough, but pretty well assured that God was going to use her in His plan."

- "We were so blessed by your ministry. Actually, our third adopted child, Allyson Joy, joined our family partly due to your ministry of *Choose Life* license plates. After buying the plates for our cars almost three years ago, we received a note from Adoption by Shepherd Care thanking us for supporting adoption in Florida. God brought this agency to our minds again when we felt Him calling us to adopt another child. Several months later they placed His precious "gift of life" into our arms. We might not have ever known about their agency if we hadn't bought our *Choose Life* tags! God is so good!"

It is a matter of record that *Choose Life* license plates have been the fulfillment of an amazing vision. Russ and Jill Amerling are National Publicity Coordinators for Choose Life America, Inc. They have received:

The Heartbeat Servant Leader Award from Heartbeat International, The Children First Foundation's first Annual Choose Life Award, and the Daniel Webster Award given by the Florida Family Policy Council for outstanding and principled leadership in promoting pro-life and pro-family public policy in Florida.

As they travel nationally, Russ and Jill, The "Johnny Appleseeds" of the *Choose Life* license plate in America, help groups and individuals obtain the *Choose Life* license plate for their state.

Do you have yours yet? Do the cars in your church parking lot display them? Do you want to help in this effort? Get your plate and donate to the cause. See below.

Choose Life America, Inc. is an IRC 501 (c3) organization and donations are tax deductible. One hundred percent of funds received are used to promote the *Choose Life* License Plate effort. There are no salaries; everyone is a volunteer. Funds from the sale of the *Choose Life* plate in each state go to support their life-affirming pregnancy-resource centers, maternity homes, and certain non-profit adoption agencies.

Donations are welcome, payable to:

Choose Life America, Inc.
PO Box 830152
Ocala FL 34483
http://www.choose-life.org/donate.php
Phone: 877-454-1203 or Cell 352-624-2854

CHAPTER 27

The Answer to the Aging Pro-Abortion Movement
Bryan Kemper

Bryan saw pain written on the faces of a few women, obviously post-abortive, as they swore at his youth group's display showing the sanctity of life. Pro-lifers have learned to recognize that *look*.

"Appalling," "disgusting," "sick," were a few of the epithets scoffed by some *older* women when passing beautiful pictures of children developing in the womb. The Annual Strawberry Festival, Troy, Ohio, draws folks of all ages, and Stand True Ministries, a pro-life organization of young people had placed their display prominently next to a popular donut shop.

Their leader, Bryan Kemper, watched as a grandma, mumbling curses, strolled by with her young granddaughters. He wondered, *how can she look at her beautiful grandchildren and still support the killing of innocent babies?* His heart broke. "These older women had gotten so wrong what we celebrate. How could their generation...?"

Mothers walked their children down the line and explained how *they* developed in their mommy's womb. Bryan saw hundreds of pregnant women excited to point out how far along they were and show everyone what their baby looked like. Not one person proclaimed what stage their fetus was, but "This is how big he/she is now."

When Bryan blogged about the event in Troy, one lady commented, "I cringe every time I see or hear Gloria Steinem mentioned. The degradation of women, children, and family was the result of the Feminist movement. I count on the fact that as this older population dies out, so too will the cries, "My body, my choice," and all those ugly *Keep Abortion Legal* signs will be reviled as much as a KKK-hooded garment."

In 1987, Bryan started his work in the Christian music industry. He determined to be a rock star, stand on a stage, and share his testimony between songs. God had other plans. Six years later, Bryan combined his passion for music and pro-life into one organization, Rock For Life.

Onstage, Bryan has shared his testimony with a variety of audiences in the U.S. and internationally. An articulate and compelling orator, he speaks at high schools and universities around the world, including Harvard, Princeton, Notre Dame, Queens in Northern Ireland, Cardiff University in Wales, and many more. His pro-life message has been heard in Ireland, Australia, Scotland, and Austria, among others.

In the past, he was a regular guest on Bill Maher's television show *Politically Incorrect* and co-hosted his own call-in cable show in Portland, Oregon. Featured on MTV, radio, newspapers, and magazines, he's made the cover of *The New York Times* and had a six-page layout in *Swing Generation*. Three documentary movies have highlighted Bryan's accomplishments.

Bryan is also an author. His first book, *Social Justice Begins in the Womb,* was released in January of 2010 by Clay Bridges Publishing. His articles have appeared in many magazines and pro-life publications. A group called Poetic Justice incorporated him as somewhat of a "beat poet." His outreach goes beyond Christian venues. His poems and songs are mostly centered on the issue of pro-life. Like everything else he does, they rock with passion.

Reaching out to young people, Bryan has spent years, encouraging this generation to get involved. Now, he endeavors to continue that outreach with Stand True Ministries. Stand True is an organization that believes the only way to stop abortion is to call out to Jesus and share His love with the nation. It asks of young people, "Will you stand?" This, Bryan has chosen. He can only hope and pray others will too.

Annual youth-oriented events are: Pro-Life Day of Silent Solidarity, White Rose Project, and Stand True Summer Mission Trip. Full information can be found on the website, www.standtrue.

The Pro-Life Day of Silent Solidarity has grown to one of the largest pro-life events in the world. Over 250,000 students from over 4,800 campuses in twenty-eight countries participated in 2011.

Usually, Stand True spends the summer on the road, traveling across the United States, and setting up pro-life booths at music festivals along the way. Every year they see more and more local pro-life organizations involved, assuring them that if they are not present, the pro-life message will still go out. There's no pride of ownership. Simply put, they can work on a new vision for the summer.

During their White Rose Pro-Life 2012 Summer Project, they had a peaceful, prayerful presence in front of Martin Haskell's abortion clinic in Kettering, OH. (Haskell originated the notorious partial-birth abortion.)

The original White Rose was a coalition of young people in Nazi Germany who dedicated themselves to educate Germans about the truth of the Nazi Holocaust. Significant young people willingly risked their lives to spread the truth, to be a light in the darkness. They raised their voices for life even though the penalty, if caught, was certain death.

Stand True's witness brings literature distribution and street ministry to events around the cities they visit, including baseball games, conventions, etc.

Stand True Ministries partners each anniversary of *Roe v. Wade* with the *Annual March for Life* in Washington, D.C. and tens of thousands of young people lead off with energy and spirit. They participate with National Right to Life—bringing masses of high school and college students to demonstrate their faith and passion at conventions and other venues. They promote pro-life oratorical contests for students. These define commitment, responsibility, and civic and Christian duty.

Bryan Kemper proudly stands side by side with some of the most amazing, beautiful young women on the planet: Lila Rose, Abby Johnson, Kaitlin Martinez, Kristina Garza, Kristan Hawkins, Elizabeth McClung, Brandi Swendell, Kate Bryan, and Elizabeth Hickson. These are heroines who lead this new younger generation of pro-life women. They are changing the world.

Founder of Rock for Life, Stand True, and the Pro-life Day of Silent Solidarity, Bryan is currently the Youth Outreach Director for Priests for Life. This is the generation that will abolish abortion.

Contact: Bryan Kemper
Stand True Ministries
P.O. Box 890
Troy OH 45373
Phone: 540-538-2581
info@standtrue.com
www.standtrue.com

CHAPTER 28

From Slavery to Freedom to Termination
Dr. Day Gardner

Have America's black people survived the evil practice of slavery, won their hard-fought freedom, only to once again face bondage, this time, at the hands of abortionists? Is black genocide terminating their population?

In the following commentary, Day Gardner traces roots of Black American History back to the beginning of its freedom and arrives at the present with breathtaking reality.

*****

In 1865, the Civil War ended, and the Thirteenth Amendment to the United States Constitution officially abolished slavery. That same year, a group of ex-Confederate soldiers formed the Ku Klux Klan (KKK). They were domestic terrorists who intimidated freed former slaves and their white supporters—prevented African-Americans from voting, getting an education, competing for jobs, or owning property.

A year later, the Civil Rights Act conferred citizenship and equal rights to black people and followed with the Fourteenth Amendment that guaranteed due process and equal protection under the law for all citizens.

From 1870 to 1895, many blacks gained elective office throughout the nation, but outbreaks of violence against blacks in the South persisted. By 1915, four-million Blacks had traveled north in what is called the Great Migration. They sought better jobs and wanted to escape escalated racism and violence occurring in the south. America's northern cities overflowed with freed slaves and their extended families.

Former farmers and field workers became bell hops, butlers, maids, doormen, cooks, and nannies--they shined shoes and cleaned toilets. They attended schools—many started businesses or became teachers. By 1920, African-American writers, poets and artists emerged in a period of creativity known as the Harlem Renaissance. Black people began to realize the American Dream came not only in white--but in shades of black as well.

Meanwhile, the KKK raged a lynching war on blacks in the south as Margaret Sanger and friends devised an evil plan of their own. A staunch believer in eugenics, "race hygiene," Sanger's book, *The Pivot of Civilization*, contained her solution to the *problem*. She touted sterilization of "genetically inferior races" which she called "human weeds."

Sanger associated with known racists who shared her belief that America would be a better place without black people. She emerged, the guest speaker at many events including a KKK rally in Silver Lake, New Jersey, in 1926.

In 1939, Sanger initiated the NEGRO PROJECT, a simple plan—get rid of black people through abortion and sterilization. She knew that some blacks would figure out her sinister plot, so she decided to take the plan to the clergy and charismatic members in the black community. They delivered the deceptive message to their congregations.

In a letter to Dr. Clarence Gamble, Sanger stated, "We should hire three or four colored ministers, preferably with social-service backgrounds and with engaging personalities. The most successful educational approach to the negro is through a religious appeal. We don't want the word to go out that we want to exterminate the negro population. And the minister is the man who can straighten out that idea if it ever occurs to any of their more rebellious members."

Sanger knew that we were a culturally-religious body of people. Today, black ministers, politicians, and community organizers are still hired to support abortion, Sanger's form of ethnic cleansing. Like Judas, they have sold their souls for "30 pieces of silver."

Margaret Sanger founded Planned Parenthood, the largest provider of abortions in America. Its billion-dollar-a-year abortion business thrives on blood money for killing children, especially black children.

Abortion mills continue to be located in black and minority neighborhoods and still deliver Sanger's same old message—Poor, black children living in urban areas—are not worthy of life. America would be a better place without black people.

The KKK brutally has killed about 3,500 black people since it began in 1865. Margaret Sanger's Planned Parenthood is responsible for the more than 17 million black deaths since 1973.

How can America say we are better than the regimes of the Nazi Holocaust, Darfur, Sudan, or China when we allow the massacre of America's innocent children to continue?

We must remember why the killing began—and then vow in Jesus' name to end it.

******

Dr. Day Gardner made history in 1976 when as Miss Delaware, she became the first black woman to be named a semi-finalist in the Miss America Pageant. She has been breaking new ground ever since.

Day Gardner has ministered to the mentally disabled, served meals to the homeless, co-hosted fund-raising drives, and involved herself with Diabetes medical research and education. However, it was during an unsuccessful run for a seat in the Maryland State Legislature that she learned the statistical truth about blacks and abortion, and that information changed her life.

She received a Doctorate in Humanities from the Faith Evangelical College and Seminary, Tacoma, Washington which she considers one of her highest honors. Dr. Gardner is founder and President of The National Black Pro Life Union. She founded the organization to serve as a clearing house to coordinate the flow of communications among all African-American pro-life organizations and individuals in order to better network and combine resources.

"We realize that if we are to be successful, it is necessary to share information and/or resources to benefit our common purpose. We acknowledge that the real credit for any good thing always goes to GOD–not man."

Day Gardner anchors a weekly radio program, and has appeared on FOX, ABC, CNN, CBN, The Glen Beck Show and others. Day Gardner's face is well known on Capitol Hill.

Contact: Dr. Day Gardner
National Black Pro-Life Union
PO Box 76452
Washington DC 20013
Nationalblackprolifeunion.com

CHAPTER 29

Unashamed, Unabashed Christianity
Pastor Flip Benham

There can be no compromise, no reaching across the aisle, no middle ground in the abortion battle. Abortion is a physical manifestation of the battle between two seeds—the *seed of the serpent* versus the *seed of the woman*, (Genesis 3:15, NIV). It is a gospel issue.

Because this is true, neither side will tolerate the other. When one chooses sides here, he is really choosing between God and the devil—between life and death.

This battle has been raging through the pages of the Bible and secular history since time began. The *seed of the serpent* is in absolute rebellion against Almighty God and His law. The *seed of the woman* is in agreement with Almighty God and His law. Every person on this earth must choose to be on one side or the other.

What one perceives the battle to be will determine how he fights it. What is your answer? How must abortion be ended?

Education: If you perceive abortion to be primarily an educational issue, you will do all you can to educate people, helping them realize that life begins at conception. The problem is that many in our nation already know this fact, but they believe a mother's right to choose trumps a child's right to live. It's not about education.

Politics: If you perceive abortion to be primarily a political issue, you will spend your time and money attempting to elect conservatives to make abortion illegal once again. However, politics is the art of compromise. To be a successful politician, you must compromise God's

108

Word to get His work done. This is never a good idea. It isn't about politics.

Economics: If you perceive abortion to be primarily an economic issue, you will do all you can to help those seeking an abortion to find financial help to see their baby carried to term and beyond. The problem is that most mothers seeking abortion want to get it over and move on with their lives. It isn't about finances.

Compassion: If you perceive abortion to be a compassion issue, you will do all you can to set up crisis-pregnancy centers so those seeking abortion instead choose life. The problem is that over 80% of the patients seen in crisis-pregnancy centers are not abortion-minded. Those seeking abortions don't usually go to crisis pregnancy centers. Compassion doesn't solve it.

Gospel: If, however, you perceive abortion to be a gospel issue, you will call the Church of Jesus Christ into the streets to stand in the gap on behalf of pre-born children. Only Christ's Church can crush the head of the serpent. If it is a battle between the *seed of the serpent* and the *seed of the woman*, the gates of hell cannot prevail against her. Abortion is preeminently a gospel issue.

And if this is true, we Christians must confess we have been wrong for over forty years in our fight against abortion. We must confess that, though well intentioned, we failed to love our neighbor as ourselves; we lost sight of the spiritual nature of this battle and how to win the war.

Ignoring the root of the problem, Americans have fought for the lives of children on every venue:

- Educated America about the sanctity of life.
- Plunged into the political realm, electing "establishment" politicians and conservative mercenaries to fight our battles for us.
- Given financially, over and over again, to help mothers in crisis pregnancies.
- Established crisis-pregnancy centers.

Only as the praying, proclaiming, praising Church of Jesus Christ allows her theology to become biography at local abortion mills in every city, may the battle be won.

The *seed of the serpent* wars with *the seed of the woman,* and abortion is one of its most horrible, physical manifestations. The devil

109

robs, kills, and destroys God's heritage, our children (Psalm 127). Conversely, we advocate education, negotiation, compromise, or compassion with God's sworn enemy. We've done everything but fight the devil and his lies with the Word of God, the Sword of the Spirit.

The only entity God ordained to crush the head of this serpent is His Church, not denominational, but *universal*. Now it's time we live up to our high calling. Theology must become biography in the streets before it prevails over the gates of hell. Abortion will come to an end in America when the Church makes up her mind it will come to an end— not one second sooner.

Operation Save America unashamedly takes up the cause of pre-born children in the name of Jesus Christ. They employ only biblical principles—the Bible is their foundation; the Cross of Christ, their strategy. The repentance of the Church of Jesus Christ, their ultimate goal.

"As the Church changes its heart toward unborn children, God Himself will hear from heaven, forgive our sin, and bring healing to our land. We believe that Jesus Christ is the only answer to the abortion holocaust. It is upon our active repentance in the streets of our cities that the gospel is visibly lived out. We become living parables to the Church, our cities, and our nation as we rightly represent God's heart toward His helpless children," declares Flip Benham.

Operation Save America's national projects each year bring the "Church of Jesus Christ to the Streets" in such places as Charlotte, NC, Dallas, TX, Orlando, FL, Jackson Hole, WY, and Rochester, NY.

Flip concludes, "There are no cheap political solutions to the holocaust presently ravaging our nation. Like slavery before it, abortion is preeminently a gospel issue. The Cross of Christ is the only solution."

Contact: Rev. Philip "Flip" Benham Director
Operation Save America
P. O. Box 740066, Dallas TX 75374
Phone: 704-933-3414
infor@operationsaveamerica.org
www.operationsaveamerica.org

CHAPTER 30

A Picture is Worth a Thousand Words
Rolley Haggard

Does the name Emmett Till mean anything to you? It should. Photographs of Emmett Till are credited by some with launching the modern-day Civil Rights Movement. That's right, pictures of one young man marked a turning point in racial relations in America.

How? Simple. A picture is worth a thousand words, right? Well, the "thousand words" told by a single picture of Emmett Till were shocking beyond belief. They couldn't be ignored or dismissed.

You see, Emmett Till was murdered in an exceptionally brutal fashion. His grossly disfigured body spoke volumes about the evil committed against him. Emmett's mother, against convention, against the urgings of others, chose for Emmett an open-casket funeral. By making people *see* Emmett, not just *hear* about him in the obituaries, she galvanized a population against the horrific crime of lynching.

To be sure, people had "heard" things like this before—with their *ears*. But not with their *eyes*. They had never *seen* them. Emmett's mother made sure the world *saw* what Emmett had to say—in his death.

You can read Emmett Till's story. You can watch a video summary. And you can see the unedited picture, published by "Jet" magazine. The open-coffin pictures of Emmett Till are extremely graphic.

They should be because to understate the enormity of a gruesome crime is to effectively give it sanction. By not showing it just as it is, in all its horror, we make it seem not so evil. With mere words

111

alone, it is easy for the public to remain ignorant and apathetic about even the most monstrous evils.

Such is the weakness of words. But show us a photograph and we instantly grasp the heinousness of a crime. Show us a picture and we are stirred to appropriate, even sacrificial, even sometimes heroic, action. Such is the power of pictures.

If we are going to end the heinous crime of abortion, we need to use graphic pictures.

A dozen years ago, George J. Annas in the "New England Journal of Medicine," observed that "in the debate over abortion we are all past the point at which facts and logic matter." Annas recognized a truth about human nature—we are numbed by numbers and lulled by logic. Stalin allegedly said, "The death of one man is a tragedy; the death of millions is a statistic." Sad but true. Mention "56 million abortions" and the average churchgoer hears "blah blah." He or she continues sleepwalking through the slaughter. But show that same churchgoer a picture of a tiny human violently mutilated, minutes and inches from experiencing the miracle of birth. Instantly he or she is viscerally galvanized into righteous outrage and the desire to do anything, everything lawful to end the abomination of our age.

If you want to rally sufficient numbers to overturn evil practices, it isn't enough to simply get people to agree these practices are wrong. Forty years of legal abortion has proven you've got to press them to be profoundly disturbed. A picture of a brutally-butchered fellow human being cannot be ignored. It must be addressed.

That is why we *have* to show the public graphic pictures of abortion. America will not reject abortion until America sees abortion. Until then, it will seem unreal, distant, irrelevant. If this isn't something to be overly concerned about, then nothing is. Take a look at an aborted baby and tell me I'm wrong.

The world understands the power of pictures. The September 20, 1943, issue of Life magazine featured an unprecedentedly graphic picture of three American GIs who had been killed in action on a beach in the South Pacific. Justifying their action, the editors wrote, "The reason is that words are never enough. The eye sees. The mind knows. But the words do not exist to make us see, or know, or feel what it is like, what actually happens. The words are never right."

So firmly does National Geographic believe in the power of pictures they devoted their 125th Anniversary Issue (October 2013) to recognition of it. Marcus Bleasdale stated:

> "When I first went to the Congo, I realized that a hundred years after Joseph Conrad's *Heart of Darkness*, nothing had changed....So I keep bringing back these images because I want to make people as angry as I am. I want them to know the minerals in our mobile phones or computers or cameras are funding violence. How can we make the horror stop? It begins with a photograph."

In the same issue, photographer Michael "Nick" Nichols wrote, "My pictures are about making people realize we've got to protect those who can't speak for themselves."

Nichols was talking about endangered animals. But what of people?

In the O.J. Simpson trial, the defense had argued that the photos were too graphic and sickening, and should not be shown. They proposed charts and diagrams as an alternative. But ultimately the judge allowed the photos. If you're going to make the case for the aggravated nature of a murder, words alone won't convince the jury. Pictures will.

Social evils can't be addressed unless they are faced. People need to see the photos of what has actually happened to the victims of abortion. Anyone willing to defend abortion ought to be willing to see what it looks like, and those who oppose abortion ought to be willing to display it. Only then will enough people feel sufficient outrage to make the sacrifices necessary to see this unspeakable injustice abolished.

How can we make the horror of abortion stop? *Show* the public.

If the ear won't listen—and forty-one years of tolerance for this monstrous barbarism argue that it won't—then we need to tell it to the eye. It has 20/20 hearing.

Layman Rolley Haggard is manager at a software firm in South Carolina. He freelances in his spare time on religious and social themes. His comments, articles, and poetry most often appear at Chuck Colson's BreakPoint website. He has approved this revision.

Contact: Rolley Haggard
rolleyhaggard@gmail.com
www.breakpoint.org
www.facebook.com/dubyadubya.wuuwuu

CHAPTER 31

Weapons of Mass Instruction
Michael Schrimsher

There is no *silver bullet*, no *one thing* that will end abortion in America.

However, graphic images accurately portray the humanity of unborn babies and the inhumanity of their murder in the womb are necessary resources in their defense. These pictures make other pro-life efforts more effective—as they reveal the unborn baby—what abortion does to him or her. Used wisely, images often change minds and hearts.

Any honest observer with a functioning conscience will be convinced abortion is an act of violence when seeing high-quality images. Strongly-held-but-erroneous opinions are replaced with indisputable facts. Abstractions give way to reality.

If an objective mini-documentary video of the most common abortion procedures and their aftermath was broadcast in silence during prime-time, public opinion would be rocked.

A dramatic shift would occur overnight. Protection of unborn babies and support for the abolition of abortion would rise. Instead, censorship blocks and limits exposure to television and online viewers. Relatively few have seen an abortion or the development of the baby in the womb.

An extensive photographic ad campaign in magazines and newspapers could similarly effect changes in public opinion. Today's culture prohibits it. When billboard companies have made limited exceptions, some individuals who otherwise support free speech rights, have resorted to trespass, theft, and vandalism of signs.

To reveal the truth, especially to those who make irreversible life-or-death decisions about unwanted pregnancies, creative ways around the media gate-keepers are necessary. The Center for Bio-Ethical Reform, with other groups, has pioneered and developed innovative ways to make abortion impossible to ignore or trivialize.

Huge abortion billboards placed on large box-body-style trucks travel unhindered on public roads throughout our nation. These mobile "weapons of mass instruction" drive through certain areas at particular times with maximum effect on a variety of audiences. America will reject abortion when America sees abortion!

More people need to know that over 3,000 unborn babies are aborted in our country every day. These billboards should be seen by anyone old enough to make a baby and decide their baby's fate… most middle school students, all high school students, and those in college and beyond. Expose them to the unvarnished truth.

Many men and women make misinformed decisions to abort their children. They're unaware that surgical abortions are performed on a baby whose heart beats and whose brain waves can be measured. Many would make more humane choices if fully informed. The hard truth removes their ability to excuse decisions based on ignorance of the facts.

When we display abortion images in public, some *already-born* people become upset. But we know when abortion images aren't displayed, some people who are *not-yet-born* are killed. Saving lives trumps saving feelings.

We don't visit day-care centers or elementary schools. However, younger children are sometimes present when we expose the images to general audiences. Experience with our own children and others, discloses the reaction of those old enough to understand depends largely upon their parents' reaction. Often, parents who don't tightly regulate their children's exposure to television or movies, criticize valuable truth-teaching moments these trucks offer. It's a tough job parents have, explaining to their children why evil exists in this world. Tougher still— what they can do about it.

We live in an amazingly-blessed nation, but our highest court decided forty-one years ago to make all abortions legal from conception until birth in all fifty states. Upon serious reflection, most folks should be more upset about the actual slaughter of unborn babies than pictures of that slaughter. Why not make an effort to stop the killing rather than hide the pictures, and stop maligning the messenger?

Rolling billboards are versatile tools in the pro-life movement. Their only serious limitations are money and manpower needed to implement all possible scenarios. Trucks visit abortion clinics to provide visual aids for the sidewalk counselors and those who pray. The message of hand-held signs or printed materials are reinforced. As counselors engage those willing to talk—clients and employees—abortion's tragic outcome is incontrovertibly displayed. Images of abortion victims *cry out* silently from the signs.

Likewise, the trucks may be driven on public university campuses and around the perimeter of private colleges and secondary schools. Their presence supports volunteers on campus or at entrances and exits. Passersby are more likely to accept other information once the signs grab their attention. Other effective targets for this public education project include:

- Businesses whose leaders support America's largest abortion provider, Planned Parenthood, with corporate donations and matching employees' gifts. Their stockholders and customers must be shown where some of their money is funneled.
- Churches whose pastors participate in the cover-up, avoid the issue, or worse yet—actually support abortion rights. Their members and visitors must be told the truth about abortion.
- Sporting events, music festivals, and spring break destinations that draw enormous crowds of people vulnerable to abortion.
- Major political gatherings, including the Democrat and Republican national conventions whose participants can effect abortion laws and regulations.
- Doctors' conventions where medical professionals, including abortionists, are making policy and recruiting interns for various specialties.

In each case, potential news coverage, local or national, may expand the impact of the project to those who were not present. Even if the images are blurred by the media, the message is carried.

As technology improves and costs decrease, large television screens may eventually be incorporated into truck surfaces for use in certain locations. *One picture is worth a thousand words*. One video should be worth a million.

Just as horrific photographs of the Nazi Holocaust have been seen by millions, may abortion images reveal in future abortion holocaust museums, the saddest chapter in our nation's history. Let us pray that abortion ends in America—that God-fearing people never go down this path again.

Contact: Michael Schrimsher, Regional Director
Center for Bio-Ethical Reform
CBRFL@cbrinfo.org
Phone: 407-810-3515
* www.aborionNo.org
* www.CBRinfo.org

CHAPTER 32

Babies as Commodities
Dr. Anthony J. Caruso

"Children are a gift from God is a wonderful statement taught by many, if not all, churches. But children represent something much greater, namely, *the external manifestation of the love that a married man and a woman have for each other, and their cooperation with God."* Dr. Anthony J. Caruso believes this with all his heart.

Pregnancy is not a disease nor a condition. In fact, in medical terms, it is unique. It is a self-limited time, rarely created by an external force, that ends through a process—labor—that usually leads to a happy outcome.

"A woman giving birth to a child has pain because her time has come; but when her baby is born, she forgets the anguish because of her joy that a child is born into the world" John 16:21, (NIV).

"If we were as rabbits and ovulated each time engaging in conjugal activity, or women had a demonstrable time of *heat* where they actively sought a partner for the sole purpose of reproduction, it would be a very different world."

Considering the way the pre-contraceptive-pill time has been characterized, it would seem conditions were as above. Without some form of birth control, everyone would have a super-family. Sociologically, this is not necessarily the case. At the turn of the twentieth century, married couples tended to desire larger families to have more helping hands on the farm. To overcome the high perinatal, neonatal, and childhood death rates was another pressing issue. With the advent of the 1960's, however, a predilection for "birth control" was rampant.

Into this worldly mindset came Gregory Pincus and John Rock and their centrality in this story. No two men could have impacted more the modern approach to reproduction, a literal commodification of life itself. Pioneers in the development of assisted reproduction, their research ultimately developed the Birth Control pill.

It was amazing, however, how women flocked to the Pill, almost completely ignoring the significant risks that were experienced. Early on, blood clots and strokes were seen in young women, ultimately leading to Congressional Hearings. Formulations were changed and the risk went underground.

Studies have also linked oral contraception to increases in Breast Cancer, which more than overshadow the protection these medicines give against ovarian, endometrial, and colorectal cancer. Notions that the Pill completely suppresses ovulation are false. There have also been opinions that the Pill might induce increased risks of infertility, or delay conception post-pill.

This dovetails the development of procedures to overcome infertility, ultimately controlling fertility. From before the 1950's, researchers worldwide tried to see if fertilization could occur outside of the body.

"It was not until 1978, however, when Robert Edwards and Patrick Steptoe announced the birth of Louise Brown, that success was achieved. Thus began an industry that called to me in the early 1990's," recalls Anthony Caruso.

From 1984 through the present time, the process of artificial reproduction has undergone amazing developments. At each point, fine control of some aspect of the process has been improved, and as of now, close to 50% of In-Vitro Fertilization, IVF cycles in young women lead to the creation and delivery of a child.

The prediction of a professor early in training, that women would be able to start contraceptive pills in their teen years, take a short break to undergo reproductive technologies, and have a child, and then return to their contraceptive practices has certainly arrived.

In addition, fertility can be extended. Taking the oocytes (cells derived from ovarian tissue) of young women transfers their excellent chance of conception to any one, no matter what age. The use of gestational surrogates can further extend the chance of "conception" to any two or three people, creating potentially limitless options and family structures—beyond all imagination.

"But where is the gift? Where is the cooperation? The further one gets from the marital cooperation between a man, woman, and God, the more we see manufactured life. Take, for example, the extra embryos created at IVF. On the one hand, they can be transferred, increasing the chances of multiple pregnancy, and *high obstetrical risks*. Or they can be frozen, leaving a potentially interesting conversation between parent and child about the *twins* who are still in suspended animation, or perhaps damaged and *aborted*. Or simply, the subject never comes up. The embryos, human life, are forgotten," Dr. Caruso thoughtfully reflects.

These procedures have been found to contain risks. Surgical risks comprise a small but real concern. A growing number of studies link artificial reproduction to increased genetic and physical abnormalities. Implications of this relatively new world have yet to be clarified.

Additionally, there are issues of pre-implantation-genetic diagnosis. *Self-appointed deities*, in the name of science, can now use the Human Genome project findings to develop probes against potentially any part of the embryo's genes. Sexing of embryos is basic, but genetic abnormalities can be screened, and unaffected embryos utilized. Potentially affected and indeterminate embryos are then discarded. Rubbish in a throw-away world!

All of these things: the advent of contraceptive hormones, the development of reproductive sciences, and its application of genetic procedures to screen embryos, have created a situation where pregnancy becomes a production, not a gift.

"The involvement of the Almighty is replaced by the skill of a scientist. The focus shifts from the loving embrace of a man and woman committed in marriage to the child, and its production by whatever means necessary."

The world of Natural Family Planning is a steady and small community. In an effort to maintain the call to true expressiveness of love, Fertility Awareness models have been created that seek to maintain cooperation between couples and God.

Dr. Caruso concludes, "While these models, too, can be abused, the maintenance of openness to life is paramount, and should be a central ideal for married couples."

"The secret of happiness is to live moment by moment and to thank God for what He is sending us every day in His goodness." Saint Gianna Molla

Contact: Dr. Anthony J. Caruso
396 E 17 Place
Lombard IL 60148
stannecenter@comcast.net
www.downersgroveob.com

CHAPTER 33

Shocked
Lila Rose

"In shock, I quickly shut the book and pushed it away. And then I opened it slowly and looked again. I was looking directly at the picture of a tiny child, maybe ten-weeks old, with tiny arms and legs, who had been the victim of an abortion. Right then I knew it was ugly and wrong." Lila Rose, a child of nine, had found the *Handbook on Abortion* by Dr. and Mrs. J.C. Willke.

At age thirteen Lila wrote in her journal, *God, it's time I actually do something about abortion.*

Within a few years, Lila Rose was leading undercover investigations of the abortion industry, founding a pro-life non-profit, editing a national pro-life magazine, and serving as a spokesperson for the pro-life cause.

Lila, one of eight homeschooled children, a native of San Jose, California, lives a life of intrigue and high adventure—a life that most peers her own age, now twenty-four, only read about in novels. She has put to remarkable service the talents, ethics, and deeply-held faith instilled within her family home.

She launched her first investigation as a college freshman at UCLA with friend James O'Keefe. They had met months earlier at a training session for student publications, and their shared interest in bold activism made them instant colleagues. Lila and James started a pro-life student magazine that January. *The Advocate* is now published nationally with a distribution of over 100,000 copies per issue.

They worked together to "wake up" the UCLA campus to abortion's grim reality and the university's lack of pregnancy services for students. In her first sting, Lila posed as a pregnant student, and the head nurse at the campus student health center directed her to two local abortionists.

Inspired by investigative work done in 2002 by Mark Crutcher of Life Dynamics, James and Lila wanted to find their own way to expose this corruption and bloodshed.

Months after their first investigation of the UCLA health center, they went undercover to two Los Angeles Planned Parenthood, PP, clinics.

"I posed as a young, scared, pregnant girl, fifteen years old, the victim of a twenty-three-year-old statutory rapist. Planned Parenthood's staff told me, into our hidden cameras, 'Figure out a birth date that works. Lie about your age on the paperwork. Say you are older than you really are. We will give you a secret abortion, and no one will ever know.'" (Lila was eighteen at the time.) "The YouTube videos we made of our tapes went viral."

PP threatened suit, for *privacy violations of its employees*. "With less than $200 in my bank account, threats to sue me for $5,000 each offense might have seemed daunting, but I had a deep sense that God, as He always does, would use this only for good. And, of course, He did."

Subsequent stings have proven that PP has much to hide:

- Rumors of their racism are true. By phone, James posed as a racist asking whether he could donate to PP to fund the abortion of a black baby. No employee hung up the phone. All agreed to accept the donation or find a way or made remarks, "Understandable, understandable," or showed excitement for the race-based donation.
- Sex-abuse victims, including minor girls, are coached by PP to falsify their application forms. Even the "pimp" and "prostitute," posed by James and Lila, found willing cooperation for their "sex-trafficking scheme." None of this was a problem to PP.
- PP employees have said the "heartbeat starts at eleven weeks, at twenty weeks, or when the baby is born." They have said, "hands and feet don't form until right before the baby is born;" "the unborn child's heart is just an electrical

flicker;" "the unborn child is fetal matter, an alien, a tadpole, a cup of coleslaw"—any number of dehumanizing names.

- Gendercide is not a problem. Just don't tell them the reason you want to abort your baby is because the ultrasound shows you are carrying a girl and want a boy, or vice versa. They may tell the mother it's against the law in her state, but "just lie about the reason." The abortionist doesn't care one way or the other.

After each investigation has been completed, a series of video releases on the local level stirs up controversy in each city or community as the overall national story is built. With help from close friends and Lila's always-supportive parents, she prepares a budget and project plan. All financial needs for Lila's projects have been met. A generous donor team transferred major sums to their bank account. A lawyer filed *pro bono* to obtain tax-exempt status, and Live Action was the name chosen.

To preserve their ability to operate covertly, few know the details of Live Action's plans. Their researchers—three friends who had been involved in past Live Action projects—work to chart out the investigation and develop briefs on every clinic and state. Lila researched and purchased police-quality undercover equipment and began training.

Lila has a great model for turning professional.

"I began each morning and ended each night in a hotel room, on my knees in prayer. There were so many unknowns. My weaknesses were always before me as I tried to be the best investigator possible, inspire and lead others, and know what to do myself—all with little outside help. With a support network and the Holy Spirit leading us, we had great confidence. We also witnessed literal miracles on the trips. Our team prayed in their car outside one clinic—that our metal-strapped investigators would get through the clinic's metal detectors—and supernaturally, they did."

Keep tuned to your television sets and YouTube videos for the latest breaking expose's of Planned Parenthood. Though government funding and preferential treatment by the Obama Administration has given PP clout and arrogance, their demise is certain, and Live Action by His power will prevail.

Adapted from an article, *Fighting for Life* by Lila Rose

Contact: Live Action
1177 Branham Lane, #277
San Jose CA 95118
Phone: 323-454-3304
support@liveaction.org
www.liveaction.org

CHAPTER 34

Abortion to Adoption
Claire Culwell

No one would guess that Claire Culwell survived an abortion.

Studies show that possibly one out of every one thousand babies are alive because the abortionist "botched" the abortion. It's considered a failure, because after the client pays the clinic, usually with cash, and goes through the procedure, D & C, saline, chemical, or other later-term methods, she expects that her dead baby will be the result.

Many babies survive the birth, but not the deliberate neglect of vital care afterwards. You hear stories of heroic nurses who rescued the "unwanted" child. Para-medics received a 911 call made from a car where a mother delivered her baby before she got back to the clinic. Situations like these are not as rare as one might think.

Quite often these miracle babies bear the physical scars of a procedure gone terribly wrong, or mercifully right, depending on one's point of view.

Claire has certain health issues. "I have hip problems, fibromyalgia which is a chronic widespread pain syndrome, and chronic fatigue syndrome. Needless to say, most days can be quite a struggle just to do normal daily activities. Traveling is hard....working is difficult...life is not a walk through the park."

Her big wish or big dream doesn't involve taking away the pain. It doesn't require her medical problems to subside. "You see, there are much bigger things in life and much greater purposes in life that I have for myself than living a normal or easier life," Claire plainly states.

No doubt Claire was blessed with a beautiful biological mother. But the greater gift was when God picked the mother who would raise her—the one whose womb did not bear her.

Whoever said that looking like your mother comes only from your genes was fortunately mistaken. "Many kind strangers and friends have said 'you are beautiful just like your mother.' Whenever someone has paid this compliment, Momma and I just look at each other, smile and say 'thank you.' Not once have we said, 'thank you, but…' They don't know I'm adopted."

Claire continues, "I can't help but think that not only did God know the perfect plan for me with the right family– He also gave me the amazing gift of having green eyes, brown hair, my momma's style, and a shy, considerate demeanor similar to hers. God matched me with my forever family."

Claire's birth and survival provides many unique opportunities to share her experience across America and abroad. Africa, one of her missions, has multiple crisis-pregnancy centers in countries across the continent. Her talks there have touched many lives.

Youth For Christ sponsored her Denver appearances, three to four events daily. Claire told her audiences the message of God's love and forgiveness. Youth For Christ ministers to kids in different detention centers and jails in multiple states, countries, and continents. They teach new life—new hope—fresh starts in Christ.

Claire entered a detention center in Brighton, Colorado, and spoke with five boys, ages thirteen to seventeen. With eyes wide open and smiling constantly, they listened eagerly. Her first experience of this kind, Claire was amazed by their questions. One took her by surprise:

"How has the news of your abortion survival and the loss of your twin brought you closer to Jesus?"

"I quickly learned that these young men had become Christians that very week. They had found hope in such a hopeless place. Each expressed their desire to leave jail a changed man. How neat is that!"

A sixteen-year old told Claire he had gotten his girlfriend pregnant when he was thirteen. He admitted they had aborted their baby. Now this boy has fathered a six-month-old daughter with his current girlfriend. He is remorseful about his aborted child, grieving the loss, but thankful for forgiveness and grace found in reading his Bible morning and night in his cell. He prays to become a good father.

There is another unique part of Claire's story. Like *Hanna* the main character in the 2012 movie, *October Baby,* Claire was a twin. Just as the brother of *Hanna* died, so also did Claire's baby brother. Of the two abortions performed on Claire's biological mother, one "successfully" took the life of her twin.

In San Diego, Claire sat in awe as she listened to Shari Rigby, the actress in *October Baby* who plays the part of the birth mother. Shari's personal testimony revealed she had a child at seventeen. Her first marriage was difficult. When she became pregnant a second time, Shari decided to have an abortion. Later divorced and remarried, she now has two living children and has given her life to follow Christ. During the filming of *October Baby*, Shari found healing while acting the scene where she comes to grips with the abortion–both her own and that of the character she portrayed.

Following Shari's speech, Claire stood on stage and spoke of God in a way she hadn't before. That God will open doors for her to be transparent with people. Her struggles, too, are real.

"When I stand before an audience, more often than not, I tell the redemptive story of my birth mother, her abortion that took my twin's life, my survival, and my life after the abortion. Our reunion—my biological mother's and mine—has given me the opportunity to tell an amazing story about God's love, grace, and truth." Now, more than ever, Claire knows how true God's word is:

"But he said to me, "My grace is sufficient for you, for my power is made perfect in weakness" II Corinthians 12:9, (NIV).

It can be the same for every single one of us, if we let Him work in our life using us for His glory.

Contact: Claire Culwell
http://www.claireculwell.com
Email: 16739225@facebook.com
Twitter: @ClaireCulwell

CHAPTER 35

Without Exceptions
Juda Myers

Ann's life changed irrevocably one summer night after going to a movie. She lived and worked as a nanny in St. Louis, Missouri. Her employers gave her a ride to the theatre, but were unable to pick her up afterwards because they were drinking. Around midnight, Ann started walking home. Eight young men loitering on a street corner had nothing better to do, so they beat and raped her.

Retreating into silence as many victims do, Ann quit her job and left for home. Three months later she learned she was pregnant.

Abortion was illegal in 1956, yet an emergency room doctor offered, "I can take care of it."

Without hesitation, Ann responded, "No you will not!"

Ann had been injured physically and emotionally, but her courage and strength of character would not allow her to act against her conscience. Ann's mother doubted she had been raped when Ann refused her advice to abort.

Determined to save her child, Ann found help from a priest. She delivered a healthy baby girl on Valentine's Day 1957 in a home for unwed mothers. Though this child had brought hope to her mother as a kind of redemption from an unspeakable crime, adoption proved to be the best plan.

A precious three-month--old found love in the arms of her adoptive parents. Someone at the agency took a picture of Juda during the placement and sent it to Ann. She carried that picture with her for

129

forty-eight years until her prayers were answered—that she would hold her daughter again.

Her adoptive parents, Ed and Alma, saw no flaws in Juda. They raised her as their own. Ed had served in WWII as a marine standing proudly alongside those famous for raising the American flag in Iwo Jima. God had chosen a special father and mother for Juda.

The tragic events of Juda's conception had been hidden from her new parents. Did the agency think being conceived in rape would be a hard *package* to move? Perhaps they knew that some pro-life people don't believe every child, born or unborn, is a gift from above, made in God's image.

Who determines whose life is valuable? Is it society upholding a culture of death, or an Almighty Creator? One person, Juda Myers attempts to answer that question with her life and the choices she makes.

Society targeted her for extermination before birth because Juda was cast into a special category. It was nothing she did or didn't do. It was solely because she was one of those exceptions, a "justification" to take the life of a developing child in the womb; an assumption that a violated woman must take revenge on the only person within reach. Even her own grandmother had fallen for society's lie—better for the mother that the child die.

Ann understood that God is the originator of all life. She saw her child as a Gift. The self-absorbed world sees such children as worthless and undesirable. They want to punish an innocent child for the sins of her father(s). Juda Myers' mother Ann, however, wasn't convinced. She fought for the life of her child.

Juda's adoptive family had been told that her mother died giving birth. In 2005 Juda and Ann were brought together, and they shared an emotional reunion.

Clasped in Anne's hands was the photo she had so long treasured. Curiosity compelled Juda to question Ann.

"Would you mind telling me about the circumstances of my conception?" Juda shyly asked. Stunned as her mother recounted details of that horrific night, Juda burst into tears.

Ann patted her and said in her sweet southern accent, "Honey stop your crying. I've forgiven those men. Look what God has done. He's brought you back to me. God is faithful."

Juda breathed deeply the fresh air of reality. Her value wasn't from society but from God.

With the hope of sparing the lives of others conceived in similar circumstances, she feels compelled to share her story. Juda works to restore honor and dignity to the women and children of rape/incest conception. Forgiveness and freedom are offered to women who suffer after aborting their rape-conceived child.

"Why does the rapist go free while the mother and child pay for his crime," asks Juda when she speaks to audiences? "Mothers do not deserve to be mothers of dead babies. Perhaps society has a misplaced compassion. Their ill-conceived ideas communicate that this mother couldn't love her baby boy or girl. Instead, it is just the opposite."

"Of all the women I've spoken to, each has told me their rape-conceived child has brought them new life and joy beyond explanation. And almost all the children are grateful for their life. Two people I've met hate their lives, but they do not believe in God."

Can society admit its error in devaluing the life of the rape-conceived? For far too long, prejudice has fueled the abortion industry, supported also by those who say they are pro-life. Why are the rape-conceived used as leverage by both sides of the abortion debate? Both sides seem to think there must be exceptions. Many feel abortion can never end without them. It certainly can't end *with* them.

Juda Myers is passionate about making her case. Arguments usually focus against the inability to pass a bill without the exceptions. Juda adamantly cites God's intervention with Gideon, Joshua, Noah, David, and others. "They never could have succeeded on their own."

Juda defends her faith, "God makes no mistakes. He is Creator of life including the rape-conceived, with the same value as all other unborn humans. God's purpose is that all humankind know His love, and that they love and glorify Him."

Founder of CHOICES4LIFE, (www.choices4life.org) an organization restoring honor and dignity to the women and children of rape conception, Juda is also a speaker, singer, songwriter, and author of *Hostile Conception, Living With Purpose* and CD, *God is Faithful.*

Contact: Juda Myers
Choices4Life,
P.O. Box 14496
Humble TX 77347
e-mail: juda@choices4life.org
Phone: 281-451-8460

CHAPTER 36

Quiverful
Lisa Metzger

The Church unknowingly exchanged God's truth about children for Satan's lie when it embraced birth control and sterilization.

Children were something to be numbered, planned, and limited.

Whether or not they understood it, the Church considered children burdens—not desired blessings.

When Margaret Sanger introduced birth control to America, the Church was stunned by her reasoning. In the early twentieth century, the Church accepted the fact that God alone planned and created life.

Today, a majority of Evangelicals openly accept and embrace birth control and sterilization. Confessing Christians condone abortion as an option under certain circumstances. Studies show many who obtain abortions claim to be "church-going" Christians.

Christians unintentionally put their unborn babies' lives at risk by using hormonal birth control, known to be abortifacient in nature while following the world's mindset on children.

How must we approach family planning? As with all matters in life, we should align our thoughts with God's thoughts, make sure our viewpoints do not align with society's standards, but align with God's Word:

"One of you will say to me: 'Then why does God still blame us? For who resists his will?' But who are you, O man, to talk back to God? Shall what is formed say to him who formed it, 'Why did

133

you make me like this?' Does not the potter have the right to make out of the same lump of clay some pottery for noble purposes and some for common use" Romans 9:19-21, (NIV).

When the Church believes that *humans* should be in charge, *not God,* in creating new life or no life, they assume the role as all-knowing ones who have taken this burden of prevention off God's shoulders.

We, the clay, inform the Potter that *we* will take on the burden of *helping* Him. As in Eden's Garden, the Church clutches the age-old sin of wanting to be God. The Church openly requests God's blessings— more money, bigger houses, newer cars. But rarely do we ask God for His most-mentioned blessings in the Bible—children.

The majority of the Church arrogantly tells Him, *Hands off my womb, God, until I tell you otherwise! Check back later.*

When we tell God He doesn't have our permission to send us more blessings of children, we claim ownership that doesn't belong to finite humans.

Letting God control your family's size seems radical compared to the culture's ideology. The Bible tells us we are to shine His light into a dark and evil world.

Lisa Metzger didn't always hold to this viewpoint. "Mark and I intended on having four children. This magic number of blessings was a compromise between Mark wanting two children and me wanting six."

Mark suggested, "We should wait five years to have our first child. That will give us time to bond as newlyweds before we begin our family."

Due to Lisa's health issues, they were told that hormonal birth control was not healthy. After weighing their options, natural family planning was chosen.

Mark and Lisa married between semesters of his senior year of college. Much to their surprise, Lisa conceived on their honeymoon. Six months after their baby was born, they learned Lisa was pregnant again. One and a half years after their second baby's birth, the Metzgers adopted a ten-year old from Kazakhstan.

Adoption was never in *their* initial plans. Apparently, God has a sense of humor. He moved their hearts toward His heart.

"After that whirlwind, we decided to hold off on having any more until after we could financially settle down—three children in four years—we needed a breather. When we agreed to try again, I had trouble getting pregnant."

Lisa was worried, especially given her lower abdominal pain, something she had dealt with through her teen years. Within a few months, she was pregnant. Lisa miscarried at eight weeks. Their baby Jordan Ahava was laid to rest at a cemetery near their home.

Major health issues emerged; Lisa had an ovarian cyst and a diseased tube and ovary. After the first surgery, they cancelled the second. Lisa was pregnant with her fourth child. God's hand was all over this, unbeknown to Mark and Lisa.

"During my pregnancy, I ended up reading about a "new movement" in certain Christian circles called *Quiverful*. I thought it was profound, yet odd. Intrigued, I showed Mark some of the scriptures on the subject. As a result of my study, we started thinking about what God wanted for our family. We wondered why, if we allowed God control over everything else in our lives, to live according to Scripture, we would withhold my womb from His use."

Hands off, God, until we PLAN otherwise...we'll let you know. When we really thought about it, we realized how scary it was that we were telling God (the Potter) when He could or could not create within my (the clay's) womb.

After this time of searching the Word of God, Lisa and Mark came to the agreement that God would control her womb, the timing of any future children He might give them.

Lisa admits, "I will be honest in saying that Mark was petrified with this new pathway. As the provider for our family, he had just traded his own carefully thought-out plans for the unknown.

The Metzgers adopted two more boys, delivered five more biological children and ten others went to Jesus via miscarriage. A long, hard road was traveled over thirteen-plus years.

Lisa reflects, "We look back with confidence, knowing that we left most everything to God."

Mark often looks at their children at night and tells them, "God knows much more what's best for you than I do. If Daddy's plans had played out, I would have unknowingly chosen to postpone you and you, and would never have had you and you and you...."

Lisa concludes, "Even if we don't understand why He chose that path for us. It's a trust issue, plain and simple. We've chosen to TRUST GOD! Will you?"

Contact: Lisa Metzger
E-mail: carolinametzgers@gmail.com
www.A2ndGenerationOfHomeschooling.com

CHAPTER 37

Radical Christianity
Leah Ramirez

Positioned in the red-light district of Orlando, FL, reaching out to prostitutes, pimps, and exotic dancers through a ministry called LivPURE, Resound Missions Base practices radical Christianity. It is one of God's unique fronts in the Body of Christ.

Leah Ramirez reminisced, "We started without anything... no curriculum, no marketing campaign. Our call was simple, 'Come and spend ridiculous amounts of time with Jesus.' I was honestly surprised we had thirty-two students sign up for sixty-eighty hours a week to do just that. We prayed and fasted together seeking the Lord. Divine initiatives and mandates came forth that still determine our course. We had difficulty learning to pray, the strain of relating together in real community, but I can say, *I wouldn't change a thing*."

When Leah Ramirez first gave her life to the Lord, she read a book, *God's Generals.* Highlighted were twelve people who shook their generation for God. The book shook Leah, and she signed up to be a revivalist on the very front end.

Charles Parham, one of those featured, had a ministry school that experienced a dramatic Holy Spirit baptism. If Charles Parham is unfamiliar, what about William J. Seymour and the Azuza Street Revival in Los Angeles in 1906?

Azuza's little prayer meeting awakened a generation for God and ignited a missions movement across the globe. Before the historic outpouring of the Holy Spirit at Azuza Street spread into a world-wide revival, Seymour was a student in Charles Parham's ministry school.

It was while Leah read this very same chapter on Charles Parham, the Lord first called her into ministry. He told her she would have a school in the likeness of Parham's ministry school. Ten years later, Resound Ministry School was born. Her heart and mandate is to raise up not just one revivalist like William Seymour, but many who will carry the fire of God.

What started as a desire for intimacy with Jesus has led Resound into more and different kinds of initiatives over the years:

- They serve as a justice house of prayer which means: They pray expecting answers to real community dilemmas and struggles.
- They believe Jesus is still the active Head of the Church, and the Church is to function with absolute mobility and energy in wholeness.
- They believe the Church, *the ecclesia*, is to function as the conscience of the state and society.

Leah affirms, "We refuse to stay put within the four walls assigned to us. In the words of John Wesley, 'The world is my *(our)* pulpit.'"

One of the most important initiatives Resound has taken on is opposition to abortion. They don't believe the Church should avoid political issues. Isaiah, chapter fifty-eight, emphasizes that our spirituality is determined by how we interact, not just with heaven but the world around us.

There is only one Author of Life. Anything pertaining to life is the issue of God and, therefore, the issue of His Church. Although it plays itself out in the political arena, life isn't a political issue. Life is God's domain.

"When my husband Larry and I were away for our tenth-wedding anniversary, we watched a video of "Amazing Grace," the story of William Wilberforce and the abolitionist movement. Over a period of forty years, Wilberforce fought and successfully ended slave trade in Great Britain. I was so provoked in my heart, I could not sleep at all that night. I asked, *Lord what more can I do to be a voice*? He birthed in my heart a strategy to see every abortion center in Florida covered in silent prayer on the same day—at the same time. We called it Stand4LIFE."

In 2010, over 1,800 people stood shoulder to shoulder in front of every Florida abortion mill. Babies were saved! Mothers were redeemed! Best of all, eighty per-cent of those who stood were first-time activists. Some of Florida's churches left their buildings and contended for regional transformation.

Praise God, Stand4LIFE continues to grow. The vision is that every abortion center in America will be covered with silent, contending prayer. All can participate, go to www.Stand4LIFE.info.

Resound Ministries operates fifteen different outreaches every week from their missions base. They serve homeless brothers and sisters with a weekly hot meal and community. It's called "Family Night," simple but quite effective. Their building is a couple of blocks from "the Trail," a high drug and prostitution area, where they give witness to those walking or waiting at bus stops. Every day, they see God deliver, heal, and save. They launched their church to disciple God's fruit.

One ministry, a favorite, The ByWay, reaches out to the children, extending the love of God to their families in some of Orlando's highest crime-rated neighborhoods. A significant drop in crime has resulted, and three children's churches were established— proof that oftentimes Jesus' greatest treasures are hidden in dark places.

Leah declares, "I believe Jesus is alive. I believe that He means for His church to be victorious:"

"And I tell you, you are Peter, and on this rock I will build my church, and the gates of hell shall not prevail against it" Matthew 16:18, (NIV/AMP).

Larry Ramirez, Leah's husband, shares his favorite scripture and a closing prayer:

"('How) God anointed and consecrated Jesus of Nazareth with the Holy Spirit and with strength and ability and power; (how) He went about doing good and, in particular, curing all who were harassed and oppressed by the power of the devil, for God was with him' Acts 10:38, (AMP).

"Lord, I pray that this generation of young men and women will receive your Holy Spirit and power to do good, end abortion, and send revival. Ignite the hearts of our young people in America. Let them pick up your torch of righteousness and lead the charge to see abortion ended in our day. All in the name of Jesus Christ."

Leah and Larry Ramirez serve as the Directors of Resound Missions Base, IHOP Orlando, Resound Internship and Ministry Training School, and Resound Community Church in Orlando, Florida.

Contact: Leah Ramirez, Director
Resound Missions Base
1620 Premier Row
Orlando FL 32809
Phone: 407-340-0204
info@Resound247.com
www.Resound247.com

CHAPTER 38

Sidewalk Evangelist
John Barros

Tanned by the hot Florida sun, John Barros, an evangelist and sidewalk counselor at the Orlando Women's Center in Orlando, has become a fixture on Lucerne Terrace. His public discourse at this downtown abortion clinic affirms, *"I am not ashamed of the gospel of Christ for it is the power of God for salvation to everyone who believes..."* Romans 1:16, (NIV).

He might be speaking this truth conversationally to people passing after they've left the drug rehab center a block away. Or a couple coming from the parking lot to keep their appointment. Or speaking to a packed waiting room through the walls of the abortion mill. He relies on the Holy Spirit to amplify his message.

Ten years ago, John began regularly showing up—the past three and a half years, it has been his daily post. He's eager to see God turn the hearts of many women toward their children.

Word has spread of the harvest being reaped at this place. Pro-life youth volunteers are learning while observing John's firm but gentle outreach. When he can find a spare moment, he posts prayer requests on Facebook. Given the gravity of life and death situations, many respond.

John believes he has done worse sins than these folks and would continue if not for God's Grace. God called John to Himself in large part through a street preacher; so John shares the Gospel of Life to the lost. Not in judgment or condemnation, but to warn, offer help and hope. John quotes scripture, *"The road they are on has a wide gate and broad road, but it leads to destruction"* Matthew 7:13, (NIV).

Second Timothy 2:24-26 tells us, *"to correct those who are in opposition if perhaps God will grant them repentance, so they may know the truth, come to their senses and escape the snare of the devil having been taken by him to do his will."* Second Corinthians 4:3-4 says *"The Gospel is veiled to the unbeliever and that they have been blinded by the devil."*

From these few scriptures, John declares all are in serious trouble without a Savior. He confronts the sin first which is very different from the way most counselors deal with abortion-minded men and women.

When a guy wants his wife or girl friend to abort the baby, often it's so he can evade his responsibilities. This choice leads to destruction, not just of the baby but the dad or mother as well—a trap laid out by the devil himself. There are demonic forces and angelic, *princes and principalities* to be wrestled in this horrible place. Those who believe the lies bring a curse upon themselves.

Clinic workers tell the clients, "this is not a baby yet." God's word shows us in Exodus 21:22-23 that God required the life of a man who hurt a pregnant woman and caused a miscarriage—*life for life*. God looks at each baby as a person. Psalm 139:13-14 says, *"For you created my inmost being; you knit me together in my mother's womb."*

John warns that those who go through with their abortions will surely see God's judgment. One *deadly sin* in Proverbs 6 says that *"God hates the shedding of innocent blood."* A baby is innocence personified. A baby has done nothing wrong in the safest place God provided, tucked into the mother's womb next to her heart.

We cannot deceive ourselves and think God will overlook the murder of an innocent baby, a person made in His image. Romans 12:19 tells us God will avenge this baby's death.

It doesn't have to be this way.

God has written His law on every man's heart. That's why we know it is wrong to lie, cheat, or murder; listen to that voice today. Jesus says, *"Come unto me all who are weary and heavy laden and I will give you rest"* Matthew 11:25, (NIV). "Seek ye first the kingdom of God and His righteousness and all these things will be given to you." Trust Him today.

We have *hearts of stone* according to Ezekiel 36:26, but God wants to give us a clean new heart. That's what Jesus meant when He said, *"You must be born again,"* John 3:3. After receiving John Barros's guidance, hundreds of young ladies who saw no hope have trusted God. No one has ever been sorry for that decision.

"Please repent today, turn from this sin to the One that promises to take care of you. He will forgive you all. *'If we confess our sin he is faithful and just to forgive us our sins and cleanse us of all unrighteousness'"* 1 John 1:9, (NIV).

This Jesus who knew no sin *"became sin for us that we might be the righteousness of God in Him"* 2 Corinthians 5:21, (NIV). This Jesus faced wrath, hatred, anger, and curses which we deserved and then gave us His perfection that we might stand before God blameless as sons and daughters.

John tells the ladies about the horrible record of Orlando Women's Center as well as the statistics that the workers will not tell them. But the main thrust of his message is the Gospel. John knows he cannot change a mother's mind who wants an abortion, but many others have chosen life through the power of the Gospel. God promises that *"His word will not return void but will either harden or soften hearts,"* Isaiah 55:11. Hebrews 4:12. John knows that the Gospel is what *makes the blind to see, the deaf to hear, and brings life....*

John Barros closes with this message, "Oh please, come and trust God today. He does amazing things. If you hear His call today, please don't harden your heart. Come to Him, He will take care of everything. There are teams of women who want to help you now."

Clearly, this is the Gospel message. When they leave Orlando Women's Center, none can say they weren't told.

Contact: jcbarrow@aol.com
WHOWILLSTAND.NET

CHAPTER 39

Heaven-Sent Treasures
Judy Madsen Johnson

Brigette, Dianna, Katiha, Denise, Jasmine, Jackie, and Patricia. Their ages were fifteen to thirty-one when I met them. Three things they shared in common: Listed on a census, they would be designated as minorities. All, "found to be pregnant," were thrown into a panic. All resolved to end their pregnancy.

Abortion centers always begin with a pregnancy test—standard procedure—but their pregnancies were already established. The mothers were carrying a child, a baby human whose life was about to be ripped from the womb. These women had accepted that mindset.

For over twenty years, I regularly stood on a public sidewalk appealing to young mothers, "Please don't abort your baby." I often was asked by friends, "Have you ever seen someone change their mind?" My answer was an emphatic "yes!" My *baby saves* are my heaven-sent treasures.

Our lives, the seven mentioned above and mine, intersected during the years between 2000 to 2010 when these young mothers arrived at an abortion center to keep their scheduled appointments. Only Jackie, Denise, and Patricia entered the clinics.

I shared truth with them that life is created at conception and the child's heart beats at eighteen days. Their baby is God's incredible gift to them. The harder truth of abortion's consequences—regret, pain, and possible injury I also shared.

This is not to infer it was easy. Dianna, eighteen and a mother of a two-year old, was adamant, "I don't want another baby." Katiha, nineteen, with a two-year old, seemed ready to accept help from any source. She was immature, vulnerable, and homeless. A third, all were Haitians, Denise and her boyfriend, were afraid her father would kill the boyfriend—it would have been an honor-killing for taking away the virginity of his daughter. Murder for this reason is not prosecutable in Haiti. How can one give answers to such inscrutable situations? Yet, God intervened through me and my teammate offering solutions that turned them around.

Denise showed up twelve months later at Planned Parenthood, parked her car, and came flying toward my partner and me with a smile that lit up her face. Denise had driven by on days we were absent, eager to announce her good news. She and Pierre married. Forgiven by her father, all enjoy her much-loved son Peterson. A sidewalk counselor rarely learns these outcomes for certain. What a blessed joy she had made the effort.

Brigette, my youngest birthmother, arrived at the clinic frightened and crying, not wanting her baby aborted. Her grandmother, with a gravely ill husband, was raising Brigette and her two younger brothers. Desperate, the grandmother thought this was her only option. An amazing scenario developed. Brigette was emboldened by my moral support and the sudden appearance of a group of rosary-carrying Catholics. Their priest's gentle encouragement changed her grandmother's heart. Baby Isaiah was born on December 26, 2010. God does indeed, "move in mysterious ways, His wonders to perform."

Jasmine's goal was to earn a college degree. She moved from her hometown to find work and take full courses at the university, but she became sexually involved with a man. When her pregnancy was confirmed, the child's father left. Strong willed and determined, Jasmine made a full commitment to her son when she realized the help and encouragement our pro-life ministry offered was authentic. Gabriel is now five.

Most of these women are raising their children alone, yet Brigette's boyfriend, a former high school drop-out, finished his G.E.D. and works fulltime at Wal-Mart. He supports their son financially and still lives with his family. Brigette is with her grandmother while working part time. They are now engaged…with a diamond ring. Now, eighteen and nineteen, these young parents are making good decisions for Isaiah.

Each day's counseling brought new challenges. Jackie, from the Philippines, stepped off a bus and onto the sidewalk where I stood handing out brochures. Jackie took the offered brochure and walked into the abortion center. Within minutes, she emerged—she lacked the required identification—her appointment was cancelled.

Jackie came directly to me. I sensed her brokenness. That same afternoon I persuaded her to accompany me to a ministry meeting. We prayed for her and she left with a plan for her baby. She had new friends to help dispel her loneliness. Alex has celebrated his fifth birthday. In some ways I am her surrogate mom. Jackie and Alex often join my family on special occasions.

Each of the preceding situations would suggest adoption might have been best for the child. These birthmothers chose otherwise. However, I've never met more dedicated mothers. They've assumed their maternal responsibilities as single moms and their children are first priority. God is in the details.

They had just gotten out of their van. In my usual fashion, I called Patricia to the sidewalk while her husband waited with their two-year-old in his arms. She sweetly smiled, then backed away, begging forgiveness as she was late. Two important facts she leaked to me: They already had five other children and her husband didn't want her to abort. Her husband prepared to leave the center. He pulled the van to a stop. I snatched the opportunity to share with him before he merged into traffic.

It was his strength and the daughter's implacable wailing for her mother that brought them back within the hour. I watched their toddler while Che' ran inside rescuing both his wife and his pre-born baby. Patricia wept, relieved that her hero had arrived. During her pregnancy, the parents experienced health and job problems, but they trusted God. Their two sons and three daughters welcomed baby sister, Alexis Estrella, born five months later.

One final story about God's blessings, my unforgettable heaven-sent treasures: I was running late to take my shift on the sidewalk. I nearly convinced myself, *It will be okay to drive over the speed limit. It might be a matter of life or death.* Instead, His answer came; *Jesus is with you.* As I slowed my speed, a calm pervaded my spirit. I drove by the abortion center noticing many clustered at the entrance, a clear indication the waiting room was full. I passed two occupied parking spaces, and found an empty spot as though reserved just for me. I grabbed my literature, water bottle, and umbrella, and jumped from my car in time to see two women. Apparently, a mother and daughter exited

146

the car in front. I stood on the sidewalk as they headed my way. *God's perfect timing*, I thought.

Certain the older woman was accompanying her daughter for an abortion, I initiated the conversation. Neither wanted to look me in the face. Both were pregnant. I've heard incredible stories before, but never a *mother and daughter* with dual appointments to abort their babies. I could scarcely contain my shock. Tears flowed as I embraced them.

I invited them to Wendy's for a cold drink. The older woman, her fiancé, and her daughter listened intently while I explored what our ministry could do to help. A mortgage payment was the factor upon which a baby's life, and the baby's niece or nephew's hung. Pro-Life Action Ministries provided the payment, but before the approval came, Linda called. She praised God and repented of the terrible mistake she had almost made. "Under no circumstances will I abort my baby."

Her daughter Lakisha's partner, who deserted at five months into the pregnancy, returned before her baby was born. Yet, the mother's fiancé' abandoned her. Unshaken, Linda's baby girl and grandson were born a few months apart.

I'm sure many are curious about sidewalk counselors, seemingly intelligent people. They lead otherwise normal lives, but return day after day, year in and out in all weather extremes. As rude passers-by often call out, "Why don't you get a life?" the volunteers are unshaken. These Christians have made a commitment in faith and obedience. Some sidewalk counselors are trained to do what they do. Others respond merely to their heart's tug, praying and seeking God's will. In both situations, spirit-led believers yield to the call of mercy and love. They are Jesus' ambassadors on behalf of the pre-born to their parents.

To actually experience the thrill of saving a life is incomparable. God does the saving, and we are privileged to be His available vessels.

Without the anxious prayers on behalf of the babies—personal and corporate by audible and silent partners, both near and far, our efforts would be in vain. God sees and rewards with heaven-sent treasures.

CHAPTER 40

Forty Days
David Bereit

What do these biblical figures—Noah, Moses, and Jesus Christ have in common with David Bereit, National Director of the Forty Days of Prayer campaigns? The number forty changed the world in their time. It ushered in a new era of history built on the power of Almighty God through His chosen leaders. Bereit appears to have been called to help abolish the greatest tragedy of the present age—murder of human beings created in God's image.

Abortion, the greatest crisis of our generation, takes the lives of 1.2 million babies annually. Death by abortion and the detrimental effects to the mothers is an affront to God and a scourge to mankind.

"When the history books are written, they will record what we did or did not do," Shawn Carney, Campaign Director. Our response should be, "What can I do to stop abortion?"

There is great urgency to raise up the power of the grass roots. To stand where we live, involve neighborhoods and communities. Its potential has been untapped until now.

Forty Days of Prayer is one significant ongoing movement within the many pro-life branches. It began in 2007 in College Station, Texas.

Its leaders predict that 2014 is poised to bring a major turn around in the course of abortion, leading to its eventual demise.

Some stats from the fall of 2013 Forty Days Campaign make the point: Since its inception six years earlier, there has been a cumulative total of 600,000 participants from 16,500 churches during 2,786 campaigns in twenty-one countries. 673 babies were saved this fall because Christians sacrificed time and comfort. Since 2007, a total of 8,209 children have been delivered from abortion. Total workers who quit their jobs—88—converted, now pro-life. Abortion centers closed—42—with other closures pending.

Surveys have shown nearly one-third of those who went to the centers and prayed on the sidewalks had never before been involved in pro-life activity—200,000 new volunteers mobilized, a future filled with hope. Even in communities identified as having a liberal demography, the most improbable of circumstances, there have been enthusiastic conversions.

Leaders David Bereit and Shawn Carney took to the road nationwide. Fifteen states were visited along with the District of Columbia where enthusiastic groups reported amazing results such as: In Glen Falls, New York during its first campaign, an abortion patient eager to escape after hearing the message of life, ran out of the center shoeless and in a gown. She hopped into her car and sped away.

Unprecedented partnerships have been forged among Protestants, Catholics, and other Christian groups. *Forty Days* is separate and set apart from the political scene, but Bereit told the *National Catholic Register* "We have seen more enthusiasm and more participation than in past years. People are recognizing that, with Obamacare, the HHS mandate, and other challenges, prayer is a powerful way to make a difference. People are recognizing that the local level, through prayer, is where we can make the most change."

Forty Days follows these biblical truths:

Jeremiah 29: 11, *"For I know the plans I have for you," declares the Lord, "plans to prosper you and not to harm you, plans to give you hope and a future. Then you will call upon me and come and pray to me, and I will listen to you. You will seek me and find me when you seek me with all your heart,"*, (NIV)

John 15: 5, *"I am the vine; you are the branches. If a man remains in me and I in him, he will bear much fruit; apart from me you can do nothing,"*, (NIV)

First John 3:16, *"This is how we know what love is: Jesus Christ laid down his life for us. And we ought to lay down our lives for our brothers,"* (NIV).

A former abortion worker, Abby Johnson, once the Planned Parenthood Employee-of-the-Year, said that the no-show rate went up 75% when people were praying outside. Johnson founded her ministry, "Until There Were None," on reaching out to workers inside the facilities. Her organization helps them find jobs and pays their bills until they have work. Her book, *UnPlanned* has been a best seller. She tells how Forty Days of Prayer confronted her with love, prayers, and grace during one of their earlier campaigns outside the Planned Parenthood where she was the manager.

One local leader in Columbia, Missouri commented, "I had never done anything like this before. It was scary, but I trusted in God and He sent the people. One out of every three babies were saved because their mothers did not come back. Such a blessing from God to be a part of it." Seven campaigns. Seven abortionists gone. "Eighteen months have passed without abortions."

Forty Days for Prayer, International continues to grow abroad. In the U.K. over thirty individual campaigns have resulted in many babies saved, impacting traditionally-stoic Brits. Three abortion centers have closed in London. The largest abortion provider was quoted, "Take your love somewhere else."

Around the globe, Canada, Australia, Spain, Russia, Nigeria, South Africa, Ghana, Denmark, Portugal are among the participants, and inquiries have come from Italy, France, Scotland, and Peru. Word-of-mouth has been responsible for the surge elsewhere. This claim has been oft repeated, "It's amazing to see what God has accomplished."

The three keys which have brought about such incredible outcomes will be continued and enlarged to double the impact of the Forty Days campaigns. They are:

- Prayer and fasting. *"With God, all things are possible."*
- Community outreach. Not through the *N.Y. Times* or *Fox News*. We have to reach them. It is our freedom and responsibility to do so.
- Peaceful vigil. Interceding at local abortion facilities. Yes, it works.

Forty Days uses the internet to communicate daily the testimonials, record of babies saved, workers gone, and abortion centers as they close. They feature a devotional and prayer.

Plan now to join their next campaign.

Contact: 40 DAYS FOR LIFE
1511 South Texas Avenue #335
College Station TX 77840
info@40daysforlife.com

CHAPTER 41

It's Gone
Judy Madsen Johnson

I drove through the old familiar neighborhood. The ugly green walls which once housed an abortion clinic stood without roof, doors, or windows. I wondered when the Herman Avenue residents were ever to be relieved of this painful reminder.

The demise of the Birth Control Center a.k.a. Women's Care Center, WCC began with Florida's powerful hurricanes of 2004. Was it God's wrath which had swooped down with fury against this bastion of murdered babies? No other structure on the street had been harmed.

Once, the community had felt protected by the block-solid building that the Civil Defense office occupied on their street. After the *Cold War*, this government agency abandoned the premises.

When new tenants moved in, neighbors were shocked. A calculating businesswoman decided that with an entrance to the U. S. Naval Training Center mere blocks away, young female recruits would ensure the success of her abortion enterprise. Patty Martin was a hard-line feminist and her lawyer partner provided cover against possible litigations. She also chose a doctor whose temperament matched her own, Ralph Bundy, the only abortionist who used the skill of his medical training to kill babies in that chilling place.

The Orlando Sentinel chose to feature Bundy one Mother's Day as the cover story in their photographic section. They devoted nine pages to his interview. He closed with this remark, "One of my Baptist, Bible-thumping friends just learned what I do, and she is trying to get me 'saved.' But I told her I look forward to going to hell because that's where I'll find most of my friends."

The clinic stood about fifteen feet from the street, surrounded on three sides by a gravel parking lot. After seasonal rains, clients had to walk through wide puddles to the entrance. Windows were always shuttered, and personnel were either disagreeable and insulting by nature, or trained that way.

One day a pro-lifer and her daughter stood beyond the property line and prayed for the mothers and the workers. Staffers later declared to police officers that these women had "threatened to come back with a bomb." Though baseless, their hoax sent this gentle lady to court, where she was found not guilty by the jurors. It was almost a drill for each new staffer to call the police and make false accusations. Intimidation of pro-lifers never flagged.

The Naval Training Center a few blocks away was decommissioned, and Martin sold her business to one of her employees. Tammy Joy's ownership was funded by her family—new management—but with the same calloused treatment.

WCC was one place no pro-lifer wanted to be. I organized prayer vigils in thirty-minute time slots for the annual remembrance of the *Roe v. Wade* Decision January 22, 2000. The pastor of a participating Baptist church, Warren Fox, was deeply moved when he saw women go inside for their abortions. He decided to return each Saturday morning to pray. We partnered in our commitment for the defense of the babies, praying and sharing God's love.

Beginning the following week, we started engaging women in conversation. A young mother had taken a bus and walked five blocks from the bus stop to the abortuary. She was eighteen, already had a two-year old daughter, and stated emphatically, "I don't want this baby."

Warren said, "Why don't we go get a soda at Burger King and talk some more about this?" She accepted the invitation.

Her fierce resistance finally gave way to, "I wonder if my baby's a boy or a girl?" We took her home to talk to her parents. She'd said her father would throw her out, but all went surprisingly well. As we left, I gave her a pair of yellow booties. After her baby came, Warren and I helped Diana and her girls on several occasions. Her family, though extremely poor, loved that child. Xhanay lacked for nothing.

153

Often the Herman Avenue parking lot overflowed. Drivers were sent away with a monitor that flashed when the abortion ended.

After offering help to mothers and workers alike, Warren left to finish his Sunday sermon for the following day. Our partnership lasted seven years until Warren took a pastorate out of state. A pastor who ministers on the sidewalk in front of an abortuary is special and rare. How desperately they are needed. Save the baby and the mother will be saved also, spared from the ravages of abortion. Then the matter of eternal salvation can be addressed.

Neighbors had been hostile at first. They didn't want anyone— for or against—in front of this facility. Gradually, we received their trust and support as they sensed we were there for the duration. All shared a desire to see this death camp closed.

Clients arrived two hours before the abortionist, but we had mere seconds, as they entered, to give our message. We appealed to those who momentarily would sign their babies' death warrants. Warren called the guys over. I spoke to the young women to determine why they felt abortion was their only option. When they heard the truth it often prevailed. On occasion, we delivered or led the couple, mother, parents, or friends directly to a pregnancy center open on Saturdays.

One rainy morning I huddled under my umbrella watching Bundy race his van toward the driveway. He liked to swerve as close to me as possible. It amused him to see me jump back. His aim was perfect—I was drenched as his van delivered my second shower of the morning.

"Ralph," I shouted, hoping my voice carried behind the building where he parked. "Please stop killing the babies, and God will forgive you."

Central Florida reeled from the impact of three major hurricanes in short succession, and the property was condemned. On Halloween, months after the storms, WCC reopened in a strip mall. The devil's holiday re-launched the destruction of tiny babies. Some victories are short-lived. I held a sign, "They're killing babies here." Another read, "You don't have to abort. Free Help. Call 1-800-230-2557."

An astonished community joined me in exposing their new unwanted neighbor. Mothers with small children came and held signs with me. After three years, WCC was pressured to leave, by "vote" of their neighbors.

I went back to WCC's original location a few blocks off my route, I steered my car around the curve and onto Herman Avenue. During my previous visit with residents, it had been rumored that a nursing home or a kindergarten was to open where babies were once despised and murdered. How could anything good occupy this space?

This time, I almost passed it. The site was swept clean. Level and grassy, a few scattered wild flowers grew. I breathed in deeply the fresh air of relief. The neighborhood had been cleansed.

I thought, *Lord, not just here but every abortion center in America. Please remove the scourge of abortion from our land so that soon all may shout in loud acclamation, "IT'S GONE!"*

The End

EPILOGUE

They say *"Ignorance of the law is no excuse,"* but ignorance on any account can lead to misunderstanding or disagreement—worse yet, disaster. Ignorance is a luxury no one can afford, especially in a country where our young people are at great risk. Unwed teens and young adults have been deceived by *women's choice,* by so-called *safe sex.*

Most don't know that medical inspection of veterinary facilities receive a higher scrutiny than do most abortion centers. One recent example was Kermit Gosnell's abortion center termed "Clinic of Horrors" in Philadelphia. It had not been inspected in years.

Filth, rats, and roaches infested the premises. Gosnell was imprisoned for the murder of a patient and three babies[*] born alive. He killed the babies by *snipping* their spinal cords with scissors. Eight staff members including his wife also confessed to crimes. Jars of aborted babies filled his freezer and shelves. He is now serving life in prison.

Few know that Planned Parenthood does not report statutory rape of minors by adult males. Instead, they coach girls to falsify their documents. Many states do not require parental consent. Some are ignorant that public schools with clinics on site often take pregnant girls to Planned Parenthood without their parents' knowledge. Yet, permission slips must be signed by a parent for the school nurse to administer an aspirin.

Consequences of the sin of abortion can be catastrophic—depression, infertility, alcohol, and drug abuse. Suicide rates are

---

[*] According to testimony by former workers in Gosnell's murder trial, hundreds of babies were slain by the snipping method. The documentation of three was positively identified. He killed one mother with an overdose of drugs.

unbelievable. A cycle of brokenness, Post-Abortion Syndrome, affects most women and many men for years after their tragic decisions. Psychological and emotional effects can linger a lifetime. The panacea of choice has wrapped its tentacles around the unsuspecting and the cocksure alike. Families have been weakened and endangered by:

- A new breed of widows—left behind—abandoned by the men who made them mothers of dead babies.
- Children aborted by their mothers for the mirage of love and security.
- Death over life, mortal wounds in their own souls, and for some, debilitating shame and dark secrets that never see the light of day.
- Abortion was chosen over adoption, and unborn, unwanted children became orphans before birth.

Abortion, the supposed final solution to birth control—abortion du jour; surgical, chemical, and over-the-counter morning-after pills— was chosen even when women or girls didn't know if they were pregnant.

Abortion on demand, abortion for sex selection, or Down Syndrome, or Spinal Bifida, or any other type of birth defect became acceptable. Reduction abortion—killing one twin "so the other might be stronger"—though virtually unknown to the general public has, nevertheless, been promoted.

Ostensibly to prevent birth defects, amniocentesis, an injection pushed on women thirty-five and over, poses a risk to a healthy preborn baby. Human babies are the most at-risk species on the planet.

After years of legislative battles, partial-birth abortion was banned in some states, but not all. People, shocked and outraged, raised their voices over the barbaric partial-birth abortion. Devised to expedite the baby's death during the second and third trimester, other methods have the same end result, deliberate destruction of human life. Just as people recoiled from graphic images of partial-birth abortion, other abortions undoubtedly would elicit the same horrified response if they were made public. None are pretty. Most are fatal.

Government-paid abortions with taxpayers' money targets minorities and delivers funds promised to Planned Parenthood to "help women" with their "reproductive health." Planned Parenthood lures young people away from parental authority into sexual promiscuity, sexually-transmitted diseases, pregnancies, and abortion.

A billion-dollar abortion industry has been built on "free" love and "free" sex. America has sown the wind and reaped the whirlwind during these years of extravagant excesses. An unbearable price. Over fifty-six-million-dead babies and hundreds of women have died or been maimed.

In Nazi Germany, pulpits were silenced. Are our pastors preaching this message? Or has a congregate shrug settled in our pews? Has the Church in America allowed this evil to desensitize our collective consciences, dehumanize babies in the womb? Hitler's "final solution" has been copied by the callousness of *choice*. Multiply over nine times the number of Hitler's victims, and abortion in America is the result.

When God's message lodges in our hearts and consciences, it requires application.

It's time to ask ourselves the following questions:

- *What can we do?*
- *What should we do?*
- *What are we going to do?*

It's time to stop the American Holocaust!

Judy Madsen Johnson

*****

Reported August 1, 2013 by Operation Rescue of an Ashville, NC abortion mill, *This is the 42nd abortion clinic to close nationally in 2013. (That number grew to 87 at year end.) Clinic safety regulations have contributed to many of the closings. This number far eclipses the 24 abortion clinics that closed in 2012. Since 1991, over 70% of all abortion clinics in the U.S. have closed.*

As State Legislators pass more restrictions on abortion centers, more babies' lives are saved. Many abortionists cannot or will not meet the standards. It's not enough to just reduce the slaughter of unborn humans by sanitizing the death camps. Abortion must be stamped out permanently for every tiny person.

A final reminder from Cal Zastrow, "Those who think that this American holocaust will end from their comfortable offices and church buildings are woefully mistaken. The question is not, 'What will this cost

158

me?' The question is: 'What will it cost me to disobey Christ's command to love my neighbor as myself?'"

ABOUT THE AUTHOR

In 1987, Judy Madsen Johnson retired as a Branch Manager from Home Interiors & Gifts, Inc., after a twenty-one-year career in sales and expansion.

She served on Boards of Directors with Frontline Outreach Ministry, an inner-city ministry in Orlando, FL; Christian Counseling Ministries, a national intensive therapy program, Buena Vista, CO; Shepherd Care Adoption, Hollywood, FL; and Life for Kids, Christian Adoption, Winter Park, FL.

Her mission trips with Campus Crusade for Christ (*The Jesus Film*) were to Jamaica and a training center in Thailand. Judy was a US AID Coordinator to the Republic of Belarus with CitiHope, International. Under the auspices of the Narramore Christian Foundation, she and fellow travelers smuggled Bibles to several closed countries before communism fell. She served on a CitiHope work force brainstorming strategies to help inner-city ministries in New York City.

Public pro-life activism began in 1988 when Judy was arrested during a sit-in at an Orlando abortion clinic and later, 1989, in St. Petersburg, FL. Subsequently, Judy served as a sidewalk counselor outside abortion clinics. She organized pro-life groups and held weekend seminars with outside speakers, testimonies, and workshops in her home church.

One of sixty, she joined women in Washington to lobby Senator Ted Kennedy, sponsor of the Freedom of Access to Clinic Entrances, FACE Bill, designed to keep pro-lifers off public sidewalks. Despite their scheduled appointment, women were arrested outside Kennedy's office. Passed into law, so-called bubble zones were established—no-speech zones—at some clinics.

Judy was named with other pro-lifers in an injunction that led to the 1994 U.S. Supreme Court case, *Madsen v. Aware Women's Center* (an abortion clinic in Melbourne, FL). The six-to-three decision against Madsen, the petitioner, upheld the injunction, but required pro-abortionists' allegations of violence to be proven. None were.

When Judy returned to D.C. for the U. S. Supreme Court's decision, she invited pro-life women leaders to speak about abortion's harm to women. Focus on the Family's pro-life ministry furnished the list. Forty-four came. Judy rented the National Press Club and moderated

160

the press conference. During the weekend retreat, the women held a silent prayer vigil outside the U.S. Supreme Court and held faux tombstones representing women killed by complications of their abortions.

The high visibility of this case gave Judy a platform. With Michele Herzog, she co-founded The True Majority; Women Speaking for Women. The True Majority was the antithesis of NOW, the National Organization of Women.

Judy combined her public-speaking with foreign travel experience, and True Majority obtained accreditation as a non-governmental organization. She attended United Nations' Conferences in Beijing, Istanbul, and New York City.

She published a newspaper, "Voices of the True Majority," and distributed 2,500 papers in Beijing, where Christian material is forbidden. With Focus on the Family as host, a pro-life coalition met clandestinely each evening to strategize the next day's activities. The coalition encouraged developing nations not to yield to pro-abortion pressure from U. S. Federal and United Nation Agencies. Judy and eight others were placed under house arrest for forty hours after unfurling a pro-life banner following a U.S. Delegation press conference.

As President of the True Majority, Judy gave press conferences and radio and television interviews, often outside abortion clinics. She lobbied in Tallahassee and on Capitol Hill before the Partial-Birth Abortion Ban was passed and met Senator Rick Santorum, the sponsor.

She traveled to the Pinellas Park, Florida nursing home where Terri Schindler Schiavo was starved to death. She joined other prayer supporters for the Schindler Family.

Judy helped establish Pro-Life Action Ministries' Orlando office and served on their Advisory Council. She recruited sidewalk counselors and donors, chaired fundraising banquets, gave television interviews, and presented lectures to middle-school and high-school students at a Christian academy. Judy taught sidewalk-counseling seminars and served as interim director until Michele Herzog was installed as Branch Manager.

In 2011, Judy self-published her first book *JOY COMETH IN THE MORNING, The Joy Postle Blackstone Story,* (iUniverse, Inc.), a biography about her artist friend.

Combining her writing experience with her pro-life background, Judy feels she has the credentials necessary to present these chapters from the lives of some of America's foremost pro-life leaders. She and her husband Mitch live in Oviedo, Florida. Most of Judy's five children, fourteen grandchildren, and three great grandchildren live in Central Florida.

Contact: Judy Madsen Johnson
judymadsenjohnson@gmail.com
www.judymadsenjohnson.com